D0057110

DATE DUE

8.31 '12			
GAYLORD			PRINTED IN U.S.A.

WALLACE STEGNER

A Study of the Short Fiction

Also available in Twayne's Studies in Short Fiction Series

Twayne publishes studies of all major short-story writers worldwide. For a complete list, contact the Publisher directly.

Twayne's Studies in Short Fiction

Gary Scharnhorst and Eric Haralson,
General Editors

WALLACE STEGNER
Stanford University News Service

WALLACE STEGNER

A Study of the Short Fiction

Jackson J. Benson
San Diego State University

TWAYNE PUBLISHERS
An Imprint of Simon & Schuster Macmillan
New York

PRENTICE HALL INTERNATIONAL
London Mexico City New Delhi Singapore Sydney Toronto

Twayne's Studies in Short Fiction, No. 73

Twayne Publishers
An Imprint of Simon & Schuster Macmillan
1633 Broadway
New York, NY 10019

Library of Congress Cataloging-in-Publication Data

Benson, Jackson, J.
   Wallace Stegner—a study of the short fiction / Jackson J. Benson.
      p.   cm. — (Twayne's studies in short fiction ; no. 73)
   Includes bibliographical references and index.
   ISBN 0-8057-1669-6 (alk. paper)
   1. Stegner, Wallace Earle, 1909–   —Criticism and interpretation.
  2. Western stories—History and criticism. 3. West (U.S.)—In literature. 4. Short Story. I. Title. II. Series.
  PS3537.T316Z59   1998
  813'.52—dc21
                                      98-27650
                                         CIP

This paper meets the requirements of ANSI/NISO Z3948-1992 (Permanence of Paper).

10 9 8 7 6 5 4 3 2

Printed in the United States of America

As always, for Sue Ellen,
who has put up with me and my work for thirty-seven years.
She has always been there for me.

Contents

Preface

In 1945 Wallace Stegner founded the creative writing program at Stanford University and was its director for the next 25 years. During that time he had many practitioners of the short story as guest professors or lecturers for his program—among them John Cheever. Stegner was fond of quoting something Cheever said during a question-and-answer session following his lecture and a reading from his works. The famous writer of prize-winning novels and something like 100 *New Yorker* stories over the years, was asked by a member of the audience why he wrote. He replied without hesitation: "To try to make sense of my life." Stegner has commented, "That is the best answer I can conceive of."[1]

Cheever's response was particularly meaningful for Stegner, since throughout his life he was a seeker—he strove mightily to find out about his background, his place, and his relation to his parents, and wondered about the pattern of his life as it evolved. And to a large extent that search was conducted in his writing of fiction—one might say that his fiction was both an exploration and explanation of his life. In regard to Cheever's remark about why he wrote, Stegner went on to say:

> The life we all live is amateurish and accidental; it begins in accident and proceeds by trial and error toward dubious ends. That is the law of nature. But the dream of man will not accept what nature hands us. We have to tinker with it, trying to give it purpose, direction, and meaning. . . . The unexamined life, as the wise Greek said, is not worth living. We have to examine it, if only to persuade ourselves that we matter, and are in control, or that we are at least aware of what is being done to us. Autobiography and fiction are variant means to the same end. . . . My life challenged me to make sense of it, and I made fictions. ("The Law," 219–21)

Nearly all of Wallace Stegner's fictions, short story or novel, might be considered in this sense autobiographical, and to understand them fully, one should have some knowledge of the special circumstances under which he grew up. As a child on the last homestead frontier, in Saskatchewan, early in this century, he became attached to the West, particularly to the Western landscape, and became curious about a history that he was never given in school. As the child of a man who was always looking for his chance to make it big in the West, who ultimately became a bootlegger and outlaw and who moved his family from place to place constantly, Stegner found himself badly needing a sense of place—to be from somewhere, to belong to somewhere. And to know everything possible about that place—its history and its features. He was fond of quoting the writer-poet Wendell Berry, who has said, "If you don't know where you are, you don't know who you are."[2]

From this background, one can isolate two primary themes that run through Stegner's short stories. One is "place" as expressed in his attention to the environment. No writer has more sensitively described the natural environment as not only a background to the action in the fiction, but often, as in "The Berry Patch" or "Goin' to Town," as a way of indicating who the characters are, what they have on their minds, and what their conflicts may be. The second connected theme is that of identity. We are all practiced shape-shifters who change our roles as we change our circumstances. Who we are, Stegner shows us, depends a good deal on where we are. We may ourselves wonder who we really are or where we belong, as does Mr. Hart in "Balance His, Swing Yours." Or, like Joe Allston in "A Field Guide to the Western Birds" or Robert Chapman in "The City of the Living," we may come to regret who we have been. Just as often, as in "Beyond the Glass Mountain" or "The Women on the Wall," we may wonder who other people really are—or we may find that they are not who they seemed to be.

The other themes featured in the stories are usually connected in one way or another to these two, place and identity. For example, belonging or having one's identity confirmed in a particular time and place, as in "The Saw Gang," has its counterpart, of course, in not belonging, which leads to themes of loneliness or being the outsider, as in the poignant story of childhood exclusion, "In the Twilight," or in the story about the adult traveler who it seems will forever be alienated from his environment, "Something Spurious from the Mindanao Deep."

Who we are, our roles in our culture, has a great deal to do with the past of our culture, as well as our own past individually, so that many of the stories play with time, often merging the past and present, as in "Maiden in a Tower" or "The Traveler," where the central characters in a sudden confrontation in memory meet themselves at a younger age. In the former story, as Kimball Harris drives into Salt Lake City, the scene of his college days, he feels like he is driving into a mirage or mural and "began to feel like the newsreel diver whom the reversed projector sucks feet first out of his splash."[3]

Who we are in respect to our culture and natural environment also has good deal to do with our gender, male or female. Wallace Stegner spent a career refuting the myths of the West, many of which defined roles by gender. Bruce, the protagonist of several of Stegner's "growing up" stories, struggles to find himself in an environment dominated by a macho, frontier code, the code of the West, which Stegner describes as the myth that attributes the settling of the West to "the lone horseman." It is this rugged individualism, so damaging to our society, that is the target of his implicit criticism in "The Chink" and one of only two cowboy stories he ever wrote, "Genesis." Its protagonist, Rusty Cullen, is a tenderfoot cowboy who is taken through a horrific experience during the Saskatchewan blizzard of 1907 and comes to realize that it is only through working with other men that he can survive in such a world. Throughout his work, fiction and nonfiction, Stegner praises cooperation and values a sense of community—the real basis, he was convinced, for the building of the West or, indeed, for a peaceful and just society. When that sense of community breaks down, as it is seen to do in such stories as "The View from the Balcony" or "He Who Spits at the Sky," the resulting atmosphere is ominous, threatening.

On a broad scale, it was frequently the women of the West who opposed the code of rugged individualism and brought the West civilization and community. In Stegner's own life, he had his father on the one side and his mother on the other, and the conflict they represented to him—individualism versus community, sensitivity versus insensitivity, compassion versus indifference—became a common strand of themes in his work as well. We see it in nearly all the stories of childhood, but particularly in a story such as "Butcher Bird," wherein the father callously shoots a harmless sparrow in order to demonstrate his independent masculinity and, in a petty act of retaliation, to upset the boy and his mother.

The themes and subjects of the stories, while linked together in the way just described, are amazingly varied, as are his settings. They range from the plains West at the turn of the century to the California West of post-World War II, but also the Midwest of the prewar and postwar periods, Vermont, Florida, Salt Lake City, Santa Barbara, and Los Angeles, as well as several foreign locations, including the Philippines, Mexico, France, and Egypt. On this basis it would be hard to categorize Stegner as a "regionalist," which is the term some critics have used in order to try to diminish him.

It would be just as hard to categorize Stegner's stories by form or technique, since he wrote many different kinds, approached them from various angles, and achieved varied effects with them. One should note that he was in several ways a student of the short story, not only having taught the form to student writers, but having written extensively, more perhaps than any other major writer of the century, about teaching the writing of stories, about his own struggles in writing them, about the problems of the form, and, as a critic, about short stories written by other writers.

An important influence on his writing came from the fact that he was also a teacher of American literature with a Ph.D. from a major university, but was, at the same time, extremely well-read in nearly every period of literature. The course he taught most often was the survey of the Realistic-Naturalistic period, which ran from after the Civil War to 1920, and he came to admire such writers as Mark Twain, Stephen Crane (whose "Open Boat" I will compare to Stegner's "The Traveler"), and, in particular, Henry James. This admiration would seem partly responsible for leading him to become a realist in his own work, bucking the trend toward such modes as magic realism or metafiction. He has said,

> I do believe the real world exists, and that literature is the imitation of life, and I like to keep my categories recognizable.... I wanted [my] fictions to be recognizable and true to the ordinary perception . . . and I thought I could best achieve that aim with a method that was direct and undistorted. ("The Law," 220–21)

Also partly responsible for his embracing realism was the kind of person he was and the way he viewed life and its relationship to art:

> Literature is a function of temperament, and thank God there are many kinds of temperament and therefore many kinds of literature. I can speak only for my own, and after considerable acquaintance I have determined that my temperament is quiet, recessive, skeptical, and watchful. ("The Law," 221)

Influencing him too, besides the Realists, were the writers of his own time who had rejected the notion of the formula or well-made story, writers such as James Joyce, Ernest Hemingway, and Katherine Mansfield, who "in place of winnings and losings . . . all dealt in nuances, illu-minations, epiphanies" ("The Law," 216).

Although Wallace Stegner's writings display an almost unbelievable range, from novel to biography to history to essay, his contribution to the short story played no small part in his enormous achievement. Many of his stories, such as "The Traveler," "The Women on the Wall," "The Blue-Winged Teal," and "The City of the Living," not only won awards, but became classics in their own time. In large part his success came not only from knowledge of the form and its possibilities, from talent and writing skill, but from the fact that he wrote out of belief and convic-tion, from a fire in his belly, from a passion for telling the truth in a clear, direct, believable way. When we read Stegner, we feel that here is a writer who cares deeply about what he is saying—he is not playing games or showing off. His art was, as he has said about the writers he admired, "a real probe of troubling human confusions."

Notes

1. "The Law of Nature and the Dream of Man: Ruminations on the Art of Fiction," in *Where the Bluebird Sings to the Lemonade Springs* (New York: Random House, Inc., 1992), 219. Hereafter cited in the text as "The Law."

2. "The Sense of Place," in *Where the Bluebird Sings*, 199.

3. *The Collected Stories of Wallace Stegner* (New York: Random House, Inc., 1990), 267.

Acknowledgments

I am grateful to Mary Stegner for her permission to quote from the published works of her husband, including from *The Collected Stories*, *Where the Bluebird Sings to the Lemonade Springs*, *One Way to Spell Man*, and "A Problem in Fiction." Also I am grateful for her permission to quote from her husband's unpublished letters and manuscripts.

Pieces of the essays in Part I of this book have been taken from my articles "A Friendship with Consequences: Robert Frost and Wallace Stegner" which appeared in the Summer 1996 issue of the *South Dakota Review*; "Finding a Voice of His Own: The Story of Wallace Stegner's Fiction" which appeared in the August 1994 issue of *Western American Literature*; and "Wallace Stegner and the Battle Against Rugged Individualism" which appeared in the Spring 1994 issue of the *North Dakota Quarterly*. My thanks to the journals involved for their permissions.

Thanks also to the *South Dakota Review* and the University of South Dakota for permission to reprint Joseph M. Flora's "Stegner and Hemingway as Short Story Writers: Some Parallels and Contrasts in Two Masters"; and to *Studies in Short Fiction* and Newberry College for permission to reprint Anne Ricketson Zahlan's "Cities of the Living: Disease and the Traveler in the Two Short Stories by Wallace Stegner," James Ellis's "Wallace Stegner's Art of Literary Allusion: *The Marriage of Heaven and Hell* and *Faust* in 'Maiden in a Tower,' " and J. M. Ferguson Jr.'s "Cellars of Consciousness: Stegner's 'The Blue-Winged Teal.' " My thanks also to the *Palo Alto Weekly* for permission to reprint Don Kazak's "What Wallace Writes."

Part 1

THE SHORT FICTION

Introduction:
The Short Fiction and The Life

Wallace Stegner, one of the masters of the American short story during the first half of the twentieth century, had a storybook life. Whereas the stories he composed are usually quiet on the surface with a strong undertow, his life was overtly dramatic, occasionally even melodramatic. It was a life of accomplishment right out of Horatio Alger, except that unlike Alger's hero Ragged Dick, Wallace didn't seek riches so much as he sought knowledge and achievement. Unlike many storybook heroes he was not an orphan but he did live for a time in an orphanage; he did not spend his childhood in a robber's den but he did grow up with a father who was an outlaw.

Despite the fact that neither of his parents had gone beyond the eighth grade, Wallace completed high school and worked his way through college at the University of Utah with outstanding grades. He graduated in 1930 at the age of 20. After saving his hard-earned money to go on to graduate school, he lost it all when the banks failed at the beginning of the Great Depression. He went on anyway to get his M.A. and Ph.D. at the University of Iowa, and as a graduate student he had a storybook romance with a fellow student, the pixie-like Mary Page, and they lived happily ever after. They really did—it was a marriage of nearly 60 years that ended only with Stegner's death.

The boy who had come out of poverty and hardship in the West went on to teach at the prestigious eastern university, Harvard, in 1939. When he returned to the West to teach creative writing at Stanford in 1945, an angel suddenly appeared in the form of a Texas millionaire who had always wanted to be a writer rather than a rich oilman. He funded the graduate writing program of Stegner's dreams, including fellow-ships, prizes, and an elaborately furnished seminar room. For 25 years, Stegner served as head of the creative writing program at Stanford, making it one of the most highly regarded in the county. He taught the short story and frequently wrote about the theory of its teaching and composition. When, after a long and productive life, he died in 1993 as a result of an automobile accident, he had received just about every honor a writer can receive, except the Nobel Prize for literature. His was an almost unbelievable life, a life of constant hard work and fidelity to his principles that was rewarded, as the storybooks tell us it should be, by fame and good fortune.

It should be noted at the outset, viewing his career as a whole, that like many a fiction writer, Stegner started out writing short stories. He only went on to writing novels a decade later, and throughout his career, again like many other writers, he wrote short fiction that either turned into novels or that contributed elements to a longer work. He often solved technical problems by working with the short forms, finding solutions which he then carried over to his novels.

Stegner's writing career began in 1930 with the publication of the story "Blood-Stain" in a college literary magazine, *Pen*, at the University of Utah, although as a professional, his career didn't take off until 1937 with the publication of the novelette, *Remembering Laughter* in *Redbook*. He went on to publish stories all through the 1940s and 1950s, 58 of them in all, mostly in middlebrow magazines such as *Atlantic* and *Harper's*, and then ended his career as a short fiction writer with the publication of "Carrion Spring" in *Esquire* in 1962. During that two decades and a half he won four O. Henry Awards and had stories included in the "Best Short Stories" of the year volumes seven times. His stories were frequently anthologized and reprinted both in general collections and in textbooks for schools and colleges.

Although his work on short fiction ended in 1962, he went on to publish novels and nonfiction until his death in 1993. He said he stopped writing stories because the story was a young man's game and added, with tongue in cheek, that he was running out of beginnings and endings. A colleague at Stanford who considered him one of the best short story writers of our time asked him why he had stopped writing them. He told her, "You can't have a major reputation with only the short story." And aside from a few exceptions like Edgar Allan Poe and Eudora Welty (who gained fame as story writer rather than as a novelist) this may well be true.

Almost all of Wallace Stegner's short fiction is intimately tied to his own experiences, tied to relationships with family and friends, and tied to the various environments in which he lived and traveled. Furthermore, the chronology of composition of the stories roughly matches that of his life, so that in reviewing his short fiction, its themes and techniques, it is most convenient to deal with it in the context of his life. However, there are a few exceptions to chronology in the discussion of the stories that follows, jumps from an earlier to a later time that are occasioned by following a theme through more than one period of his life.

The Early Stories:
Saskatchewan—the Last Plains Frontier

Wallace Stegner's father and mother were married and lived in Grand Forks, North Dakota, but his mother, Hilda Paulson Stegner, went back to her family's farm near Lake Mills, Iowa, to give birth to her second son, who was born on February 18, 1909. Wallace's writing later in life would be heavily influenced by the lives and characters of both his father and mother. His father was a "boomer," always looking for the main chance to get rich, a man, according to his son, who was born a hundred years too late to cash in on the westward expansion. George Stegner had all the frontier skills, but there was no longer any real frontier to go to. He was a tough taskmaster, who knocked around his younger son when angry, and gave most of his attention to Wallace's older brother, Cecil, who was a promising athlete. By contrast to Cecil, Wallace was, as he recalls, "a shrimp." Worse, he had a circulation problem that made it impossible for him to get his hands warm in the cold climates where they lived. So as far as his father was concerned, Wallace was a crybaby, always complaining and never meeting the challenge "to be a man."

Wallace's mother was a different matter. She, too, led a life unfulfilled, but all she wanted was to be able to settle down in a house of her own, to raise her children, and to be able to have friends. Her husband's frequent moves in his search for the "Big Rock Candy Mountain" (Stegner's metaphor for striking it rich) and his activities outside the law made having friends and a settled life impossible. She was a loving, kind, and generous woman who encouraged Wallace's interest in books, supported him in his effort to achieve in school, and defended him, as much as she was able, from her husband's rages. Her younger son ended up thinking of her as a saint.

It was a rough life. When Wallace was three, George moved his family to a logging camp in what is now Redmond, Washington in preparation for going on to the gold rush in Alaska, but Wallace came down with scarlet fever, forcing his father to postpone the journey north—another cause for resentment. George opened a lunch counter for loggers, but that was only a temporary occupation while he looked around for another opportunity. That came when he heard about the opening up of homesteads in Saskatchewan and the possibility of making money on wheat, which was escalating in value because of the First World War. He took off to investigate, leaving his family, nearly penniless, behind. It was at this point that Wallace and his brother were given over reluctantly to an orphanage in Seattle by their mother who could not earn enough money to support herself and her children. As soon as she realized how terrible conditions in the orphanage were, however, she took her boys out and, with some embarrassment, went back to the family farm and to the father in Iowa who had disapproved of her marriage.

Eventually George sent for them, and in the spring of 1914 Hilda, Cecil, and Wallace traveled by train and then wagon to Eastend, Saskatchewan, a railroad camp that was little more than a wide place in the road. For a time the family lived in an old dining car that had been hauled to a lot on Main Street. Wallace went to school for the first time, in a makeshift classroom over a butcher shop. That first summer George and his two sons went out to improve the homestead he had filed for, located on the desolate prairie near the Montana border. While their father built a shack, a corral, and a reservoir to hold water from the wet-weather spring, and while he plowed the land and planted a crop, the boys found themselves sweltering in unbelievable heat and bored to tears. Wallace and Cecil played every two-handed game of cards they knew, again and again, and ended up occupying much of their time eradicating the gophers that threatened the crop.

Most of Stegner's early stories, written during the late 1930s and early 1940s, deal with his years on the last homestead frontier. "Saskatchewan," he has written, "is the richest page in my memory, for that was where . . . for a half dozen years, we had . . . a house of our own, a united family, and a living, however hard."[1] A couple of his stories have their setting in town, but most take place on the farm 50 miles south, out on the prairie. After the first summer of playing cards and hunting gophers with Cecil, Wallace was alone with his mother and father during summers at the homestead. His brother had found a job at the grocery store and from 1915 on stayed behind in town.

Stegner's first important story, "Bugle Song" (later "Buglesong") (1938), reflects his isolation during these summers. It is a quiet story, one that creates an atmosphere of aloneness through its very quietness. What drama there is is carried almost subliminally in a subtext of conflict in gender roles involving the boy who is the protagonist, but a conflict that he is too young to recognize. With only his mother nearby—his father is presumably out working on the homestead—the boy is left to his own devices on the hot and monotonous prairie. We see him first as hard and insensitive to the suffering of animals. He seems to perform his grisly task of trapping gophers and killing them (and on occasion feeding them to his pet weasel) with grim satisfaction as part of the process of growing up and into the masculine frontier role.

Although absent during the course of the story, it is obviously the father, or his spirit, that dominates this family. The mother protests the boy's cruelty and he ignores her. Yet he does follow her wishes in preparing for school in the fall by reading his poetry book, and in this and the romantic daydreams generated by the poems reflect her softer, more civilized approach to life. Similar contrasts between male and female roles, insensitivity and sensitivity, and caring and uncaring are carried as themes throughout most of the stories in this series based on Stegner's memories of his childhood.

One distinguishing characteristic of Stegner's fiction that appears even in this very early story is his power of description. No one has been better able to create an atmosphere or a mood, or to subtly suggest a condition of the soul or spirit, by providing a suggestive landscape. Take for example, the opening of "Bugle Song":

> There had been a wind during the night, and all the loneliness of the world had swept up out of the southwest. The boy had heard it wailing through the screens of the sleeping porch where he lay, and he had heard the washtub bang loose from the outside wall and roll down toward the coulee, and the slam of the screen doors, and his mother's padding feet after she rose to fasten things down. Through one half-open eye he had peered up from his pillow to see the moon skimming windily in a luminous sky; in his mind he had seen the prairie outside with its woolly grass and cactus white under the moon, and the wind, whining across that endless oceanic land, sang in the screens, and sang him back to sleep.[2]

Here the sound of the wind defines immediately the relationship of the boy to his surroundings—only his mother is there to "fasten things down." The sounds of the washtub and screen doors banging underscore the threat of emptiness suggested by the wail of the wind. After the intercession by the mother, the character of the wind changes; the boy is reassured, as the wind sings him back to sleep. Not only is the condition of the boy defined, but the role of the mother—omnipresent, protective—is indicated as well. After she ties things down the imagery is softened so that we see the moon in a "luminous sky" and underneath, the "woolly grass" and the cactus made white, a transformation in the boy's mind's eye that connects with his later romantic daydreams. These are inspired by the "snowy mountains to the south" that he can barely see in the distance over the prairie. These images in turn are connected to his favorite poem that speaks of "snowy summits" of castle walls. But aside from such messages about the boy's situation and desires, the quality of this opening paragraph that strikes us most immediately is its haunting beauty.

Wallace's emotional isolation and feelings of deficiency and failure in childhood had a profound effect in the formation of the outlook and values held later in life, particularly his concern for community, and in his selection of his subjects and themes for his writing. No story tells more graphically the pain and embarrassment of being an outsider than another one in this series, "In the Twilight" (1941). It concerns the young boy, now called Bruce, who is determined to prove his manliness by remaining stoically unaffected by the sight of his father butchering a sow in preparation for winter. His mother worries about Bruce and his brother watching such a bloody business:

> "I don't think they should see things like that," the mother said helplessly.
> "Oh, rats," he [the father] said. "I always watched butcherings when I was a kid. You want to make them so sissy they can't chop the head off a rooster?" (140)

The mother tells Bruce not to watch, but he says, "Ah, heck," and deliberately disobeys her. He doesn't want to be a mama's boy, the worst thing a male can be in a frontier society. And because it is a male-dominated society, the mother's objections are expressed "helplessly" and her orders to her son can be disobeyed by him with impunity. Bruce talks tough and brags about his manly resilience, but despite his brave front his constitution betrays him. After a hectic chase the father is able to corner the sow and kill it, and at that point Bruce has to turn away, throwing up in front of his father, brother, and friends. He feels so faint that he has to go into the house to lie down, totally humiliated.

Everything that Stegner has said or written about his life indicates that these stories about childhood closely reflect his own childhood condition and emotions. The nonfictional and the fictional versions of his growing up make it clear that a split developed early in his consciousness between the proud, intolerant, rugged individualism represented by his father and the friendly, tolerant, neighborly tendencies toward caring and cooperation represented by his mother and while trying to follow the father's lead at first, eventually it was his mother that he learned to admire. Later, as a writer, he came to see the conflict between his father and mother as a synecdoche for the Western clash between the forces of frontier toughness and independence on the one side and the forces of cooperation and community on the other. The metaphor extends to society as a whole, its pervasive conflicts of conservative versus liberal, know-nothing versus intellectual, and the doctrine of getting-rich-quick versus the belief in service to others. It may seem like a gigantic jump from childhood unhappiness to adult environmentalist, but the very ethic espoused by his mother of charity and concern for all is at the root of Stegner's concern for the earth, and his hatred of his father's opportunism and greed is at the root of his resistance to the forces of exploitation.

Another of the stories set in Saskatchewan applies the values of the adult environmentalist to the writer's early life, as well as exploring once again male and female roles. In "Butcher Bird" (1941) the father, mother, and boy travel four miles from the homestead to welcome their new neighbors, the Garfields, who have come over from England. Mr. Garfield is very pleasant and kindly, but his gentle ways irritate the boy's father, Harry, who during the visit becomes increasingly grouchy. The mother and son, on the other hand, are charmed by the man's courtesy and hospitality—the Garfields serve lemonade and play their gramophone, and Mr. Garfield makes a point of talking to the boy. The mother and son are also taken by the man's love of growing things—he has planted and nourished trees in this treeless place—and his concern for animals. This is a bit surprising for the boy, who has made a career on the homestead of killing animals and who, based on his father's actions, has assumed hunting and killing to be part of the masculine role.

In the conflict between the mother's and father's responses to Garfield, there is once again a subtext of commentary on gender roles in our society. Because the Englishman speaks politely, responds to beauty, is kind and generous, and, above all, opposes the cruel trapping or shooting of animals, the father thinks of him as a sissy—that is, from the male, ruggedly individualistic point of view Garfield expresses qualities and emotions that the father (and the frontier, masculine society he represents) feels are only appropriately expressed by women. A man should be rough, stoic, and practical. After the visitors leave and go back to their farm, the father mocks Garfield's manner of speaking, his British accent, and his dislike of killing things: " 'I just can't bear to shoot anything any more,' he [the father] said, and laughed" (155). And then a few minutes later, after cleaning the .22 that Garfield had given the boy (making him promise to kill nothing but those animals that kill for pleasure), the father tests the gun by shooting a harmless sparrow, despite the mother's protests, and ignores the boy's horrified response.

The death of the bird suggests the antilife, antilove force of traditional male values and the American frontier belief that nature was created for man's use—or even his impulsive abuse. Patriarchal control not only extends over the family but attempts to subordinate surrounding nature as well. Nothing soft, gentle, harmless, or beautiful should survive. All that counts is the physical strength that provides control. This mind-set stands for all the negative human qualities that Stegner would resist. It represents the arrogance that has allowed men to carelessly despoil the land. It represents the greed and competition that invariably lead to cruelty, violence, and war. Throughout Stegner's work, in opposition to this pattern, it is womankind that is most likely to represent the best in humanity. The boy's challenge as we see him grow up in these stories is to learn to resist uncaring toughness and embrace the best in humankind, to resist cultural and peer pressure in order to define his own caring individuality.

Male violence is central to a pair of stories in this cycle, "Goin' to Town" (1940) and "Two Rivers" (1942). It looms in the background of both like a dark shadow, an omnipresent threat to the sensitive boy. "Goin' to Town" begins with great joy, but as the story goes forward, the shadow grows, and the atmosphere changes from joy in the morning, hope, joking, eagerness and affection, to hopelessness, anger, blame, defeat, churlishness, and, finally, physical violence. It is a painful tale of childhood disappointment.

The family has planned for a great outing, a relief from the dreary emptiness and dull routine of prairie farm life during a hot summer. They plan to travel to the nearest town (south in Montana) on the Fourth of July, witness a baseball game, see the fireworks, hear the band, watch the parade, drink lemonade, and eat ice cream. The boy has been promised that he will have a paper horn to blow. But the old car won't start. The father cranks and cranks, harder and harder, until he is covered with sweat and nearly exhausted. The mother begins to fuss and nag, "I don't see why you didn't make sure last night." The boy, worried, "stood on one foot, then on the other, time pouring like a flood of uncatchable silver dollars through his hand" (79).

The father, under pressure from his wife and son, becomes more and more frustrated. He cleans the ignition points and spark plugs. He jacks up the rear wheel. Finally, at the mother's suggestion, they hook up the team of horses to the car and haul it, plunging and choking, around the backyard in an effort to get it started. Stegner describes the scene as no one else, except perhaps Faulkner, could have described it:

> And the galloping—the furious, mud-flinging, rolling-eyed galloping around the circle already rutted like a road, the Ford, now in savagely held low [sic], growling and surging and plowing behind; the mad yapping of the dog, the erratic scared bursts of runaway from the colt, the mother in sight briefly for a quarter of each circle, her hands to her mouth and her eyes hurt, and behind him in the Ford his father in a strangling rage, yelling him on, his lips back over his teeth and his face purple. (83)

Then it is over—failure. The boy begins to blubber and the father explodes: "All the fury of a maddening morning concentrated itself in a swift backhand blow that knocked the boy staggering" (83).

Typical of a Stegner story, there is not a plot in the ordinary sense but rather an emotional progression—in this case, from early morning joy to anger and then disappointment—a progression that is carried in both the story's imagery and its rhythmic patterning. The story begins quietly in early morning of a day that has been anticipated for weeks. At the edge of the dooryard, the boy, who can't wait for the day to start and is the first one up, smells the air—so fresh after the night's rain—and his mood is suggested when he sniffs at it as he "would have sniffed at the smell of cinnamon" (75). Feeling the mud under his toes, he presses his foot down and lifts it up to see the neat imprint of his instep and the five dots of his toes. These gestures suggest a vital, sensory connection between the boy and his surroundings, and as he stands in the dim morning light, he feels his own "verticality in all that spread of horizontal land" (75). His spirit soars. He feels immense: "A little jump would crack his head on the sky; a few strides would take him to any horizon" (75).

But as things begin to go wrong, the atmosphere gradually changes to frustration and anger, and each step downward, like the accelerating beat of a tom-tom, increases the story's intensity, so that with the circling of the horse-drawn car in a futile effort to get it started, ever faster and emotionally draining, a climax is reached. The boy's crying comes at a moment when the father can't take the strain anymore. The tension in the family (and for the reader) bursts as "all the fury of a maddening morning concentrated itself" in the father's backhand blow. The mother comforts her son and scolds the father, "As if he wasn't hurt enough already!" (84).

The boy's condition, his hurt, sadness, and at last resignation, is suggested in a series of metaphors that circle back to the beginning of the story. As he looks out toward the horizon and searches for a watermark, he can see nothing but waves of heat: "The horizon was a blurred and writhing flatness where earth and sky met in an indistinct band of haze. This morning two strides would have taken him there; now it was gone" (84). Reduced in spirit as well as stature and looking down, he sees the clean footprint that he had made in the early morning. Aimlessly, he puts one foot down one after the other on the still-moist ground, forming a circle six feet in diameter "of delicately exact footprints, straight edge and curving instep and the five round dots of toes" (84). The circle of the day, the circle of the horses, the circle of emotions, and the circular structure of the story all come together in the lonely figure of the boy, who, as in the beginning, is joined to the earth.

The circle which closes at the end of this story is a diagram, in more obvious form than usual, of the typical Stegner story pattern. In giving a reading from his *Collected Stories* at a bookstore in Northern California, he said,

> I don't have any formula or theory of the short story. The only thing I do demand of a short story, my own or anyone else's, is that it ought to close some sort of circuit—a plot circuit, an emotional circuit, psychological circuit, a circuit of understanding, so in the end there is some sense of completion.[3]

Most of Stegner's stories are carefully structured. His building blocks are metaphors, which in turn carry the emotions of the story, and his themes are usually expressed by means of an emotional progression, up or down, that leads to some kind of insight or epiphany that is in itself embodied in figurative language. One might say that his collected stories form a series of "realizations" about the world, about living, about relationships. Sometimes the realization is a grim one, sometimes sunny and buoyant. But no matter what the emotion of the ending, there is always a sense of morality, of right conduct, that accompanies it. Sometimes that sense is front and center, but other times it is only hinted at a whiff that we are only barely conscious of, a touch like a sudden temperature shift of only a couple of degrees.

Such subtlety characterizes the slight shadow that intrudes on the companion story to "Goin' to Town," "Two Rivers," which takes place the next day on the same homestead farm. The boy is still smarting from the slap his father gave him in response to his "blubbering." It is even clearer in this story how the patriarchal father serves as the thermostat of the family's emotional situation; they must "read" him to know where they stand and how to relate to him and to each other. On this day, the reading is well into the comfort zone. Unlike the previous day, the father has gotten up first in anticipation of making amends for the family's disappointment. The boy learns that they are going to go on a picnic into the mountains and finds that the car is already packed and ready to go:

> All his sullenness gone now, the boy said, "When did you get all this ready?"
> His father grinned. "While you slept like a sluggard we worked like a buggard," he said. The boy knew that everything was perfect, nothing could go wrong. When his father started rhyming things he was in his very best mood, and not even breakdowns and flat tires could make him do more than puff and blow and play-act. (117)

If in the first story everything went wrong, now everything goes right.

Despite the upbeat nature of the story on its surface, it is one, like many of Stegner's stories, with sinister overtones that although slight, the reader is still clearly meant to feel. All this happiness and joy feels so tenuous, coming out of the male patriarch who sets the emotional agenda—neither the boy nor the mother have much to say about whether it is going to be a good day or bad. Indeed, the mother is reduced to her traditional role in these stories as intermediary: she enjoys the day, but we are aware that she is very concerned that everyone gets along and that nothing comes up to set the father off in the wrong direction. Somewhat more sinister is the boy's memory of another excursion years earlier, a sketchy remembrance accompanied by "things that made his skin prickle," things unnamed and certainly ominous. We wonder, is this another occasion, as dramatized in "Goin' to Town," when the father lost his temper and things so terrible happened that the boy has repressed the memory of them? The boy can't quite recall what happened on that other day, but it was "something bothersome and a little scary." As he sits on a ledge in the mountains and looks outward, he senses the memory:

> [O]ver the whole canyon, like a haze in the clear air, was that other thing, that memory or ghost of a memory, a swing he had fallen out of, a feel of his hands sticky with crushed blackberries, his skin drinking cool shade, and his father's anger—the reflection of ecstasy and the shadow of tears. (123–24)

The story is not just about gender differences or mood and how our emotions can affect the emotions and well-being of those around us. It turns to other, related themes—the emotions we invest in places, the individuality of memory, and a favorite Stegner topic, identity and whether we really can know other people. The boy's mother remembers a bear intruding into that picnic day of the past, but there was no bear in his memory, only those vague feelings that make his skin prickle. His mother looks at him, puzzled,

> "It's funny you should remember such different things than we remember," she said. "Everything means something different to everybody, I guess." She laughed, and the boy thought her eyes looked very odd and bright. "It makes me feel as if I didn't know you at all," she said. (125)

For the most part, life in Saskatchewan on what Stegner has called "the last homestead frontier in North America" was hard. His father worked from dawn to dark on the land during the summers and had only one really successful wheat crop for six years of strenuous effort. During the winters he worked at various jobs and money-making ventures in town, including playing poker and then bootlegging. There had to be some way to make a living. Although there was only one working ranch in the vicinity of Eastend, Wallace and the other children of the frontier found their role models there:

> It was the cowboy tradition, the horseback culture, that impressed itself as image, as romance, and as ethical system upon boys like me. . . . Many things that those cowboys represented I would have done well to get over quickly, or never catch: the prejudice, the cal-

lousness, the destructive practical joking, the tendency to judge everyone by the same raw standard.[4]

That code of cowboy behavior came into conflict with his basic
decency even as a young child, but he felt helpless to resist in the face of
overwhelming peer pressure to conform. When he was 10 or 11, Wallace
became friends with a Chinese cook by the name of Mah Li, who was
constantly being victimized having his pigtail pulled or his shirttails set
on fire. Although Wallace considered Mah Li a friend, the pressure to go
along with the gang was too much for him—particularly since Wallace
himself was fighting the label of weakling and crybaby—and he "would
have been ashamed not to take part in the teasing, baiting, and candy-
stealing that made . . . [Mah Li's] life miserable" (*Wolf Willow*, 139).
Having given way to peer pressure, Wallace later came to regret the
betrayal of his friendship, his behavior haunting him until he exorcised
it in a story called "The Chink" (1940). The opening lines are telling:
"After almost a quarter of a century I still remember Mah Li better than
I can remember anyone else in that town" (*Collected Stories*, 191). In the
fiction Mah Li is a Chinese laundryman and truck gardener who deliv-
ers vegetables to the boy's family and who befriends the boy. He is
cheerful and agreeable, a hard worker but a lonely outsider who never
really becomes acclimated to the white man's world.
As time goes by, the boy becomes more and more friendly with the
Chinese gardener, although they communicate more with gestures than
by language, and Mah Li through example, rather than words. But the
boy still shares the community's prejudice to some extent and doesn't
really think of Mah Li and his brother, Mah Jim, as human beings. Then
one day the boy hangs around the brothers' garden, and Mah Li gives
him a vine-ripened tomato:

> I remember how heavy and sun-warmed the tomato was, and how I had
> to jump backward and stick out my face because the juice spurted and
> ran down my chin when I bit into it. We stood in the plant-smelling
> garden, under the yellow summer hills, with the sun heavy and hot on
> our heads, and laughed at each other, and I think that's where I first
> found out that Mah Li was human. (193)

But despite the growing affection between the two, on Halloween
the boy is part of a gang that turns over the Chinese brothers' outhouse,
with one of the brothers in it. The boy thinks it is Mah Jim, but it is

Mah Li. Finally, after several opportunities—to stop the prank, to report the problem to the authorities—the boy discovers his friend in the outhouse, unconscious. In part the boy was delayed in helping Mah Li by the outbreak of the 1918 flu, but mostly it is his hesitation to go against the group that prevents the boy from checking on his Chinese friend sooner. Mah Li is dead and Mah Jim will go back to China. The story is one that will break the reader's heart without resorting to sentimentality. It follows very closely what Stegner has told us happened in life, and we can infer that a hard lesson had to be learned: the pain of being scorned by the group is neither as deep nor as long lasting as the realization that one has done the wrong thing by going along with the group. In looking back, the author could see that he was led astray by what he later was able to identify as the callous frontier values of that time and place. He had participated in his own "Oxbow Incident" as a child and lived on to regret it, a regret that would contribute to one of his major preoccupations as a writer.

Western Mythology and
Stories Related to Adolescence

As we have seen in these early stories dealing with his childhood experiences, Stegner introduces a theme, opposition to "rugged individualism" (a phrase coined by Herbert Hoover), that he would pursue throughout his career. He would condemn the doctrine as false and dangerous and see its pervasive influence in our society, particularly in the West, and its persistence into the late twentieth century as signs that our society had not yet grown up. For Stegner, the West was not settled and built by the lone adventurer on horseback; social maturity involved cooperation and required the individual's assumption of responsibility to others.

The emblem of rugged individualism has been the lonely cowboy, nowadays known around the world as the Marlboro man. Stegner explored the creation of the cowboy myth in his introduction to Ben Vorpahl's *My Dear Wister—The Frederic Remington-Owen Wister Letters*:

> In [these] pages we watch the complete, triumphant ontogeny of the cowboy hero, the most imagination-catching and durable of our mythic figures. Owen Wister and Frederic Remington, whose collaboration is the subject of Ben Vorpahl's study, create him before our eyes. They begin to mold him out of the observed realities of the brief, furious, passing empire of the cattlemen. They shape him by imitation and trial and error into the hero of a romantic fiction, and in the process they are themselves shaped, as the cowboy image is, by the torque of an anonymous, public, everywhere-and-nowhere myth-making impulse. Believing they record reality, they helplessly remade it larger than life, until when they are done their creation rides off the pages into the sunset of a thousand horse operas, the free, lonely, self-reliant, skilled, eternally ambiguous embodiment of a national, indeed a human, fantasy.[5]

The cowboy myth has implications that have run deep in our culture. It has largely provided our archetype for manhood, the cowboy with his six-shooter (or one of his descendants, Rambo with his AK-47) that most young boys are led to emulate starting at three and four years old. Following the "frontier tradition" and "code of the West," they learn to exclude girls from their play as incompetent, and they are taught by their culture—usually regardless of how pacifistic their parents may be—that violence is an essential part of the masculine role. Our love of guns also runs very deep since it defines who we, as males, are (and what we are as Americans). This too is a remnant of the frontier and our retrospective response to the mythic glow that clings to that period of our history.

The "romance" of the old West, with its associated mythology, has corrupted our values and distorted our perspective to an unbelievable extent, far more than most people realize. In his essay "Variations on a Theme by Crevecoeur," Stegner cites the saga of the survivalist Claude Dallas, who killed two Idaho game wardens a number of years ago when they caught him poaching:

> For months, until he was captured early in 1987, he hid out in the deserts of Idaho and Nevada, protected by people all over the area. Why did they protect him? Because his belated frontiersman style, his total self-reliance and physical competence, his repudiation of any control, appealed to them more than murder repelled them or law enlisted their support.[6]

Did Dallas shoot these men in a chivalric duel, a walk-down out of *The Virginian?* Was he correcting injustice, rescuing fair maiden, or punishing social evil? No—he was avoiding payment of a small fine. He shot the two wardens from ambush and then coolly walked up to them and one at a time finished them off with a bullet in the back of the head. When this kind of behavior is not only approved of but implicitly encouraged by a significant number of people in an area, there would seem to be a screw loose in our society.

Stegner's adherence to the realistic mode of writing came out of his opposition to such destructive myths as the heroic lone gunman. It also came out of his need to discover who he was—his roots and the real nature of his home territory. The only two cowboy stories that he ever wrote demonstrate his realism, as well as his need to discover and set down the history of the place where he grew up. The first of these stories, "Genesis," is a particularly strong myth-buster, about as unromantic as a story about cowboys could be. First published in *Contact* in 1959, it was later included in Stegner's history-memoir called *Wolf Willow* (1962) and finally in *Collected Stories* (1990).

"Genesis" is fictionalized history, the story of the death and destruction on the cattle ranches in Stegner's part of Saskatchewan during the terrible winter of 1906–1907. It is also a story of survival, the survival of a tenderfoot Englishman, Rusty Cullen, who with certain vague romantic expectations has joined up to become a ranchhand and who learns that in this time and place "what would pass for heroics in a softer world was only chores." In a futile effort to round up as many cattle as possible before they freeze, the drovers are caught in a blizzard so fierce that they barely manage to save themselves. They do so after great effort and much suffering, but only by group effort, by cooperation and sacrifice for others. No one of them could have made it alone. Rusty Cullen's thoughts at the end of his ordeal summarize Stegner's thoughts about the frontier as it really was experienced:

> The Rusty Cullen who sat among them was a different boy, outside and inside, from the one who had set out with them two weeks before. He thought that he knew enough not to want to distinguish himself by heroic deeds: singlehanded walks to the North Pole, incredible journeys, rescues, what not. Given his way, he did not think that he would ever want to do anything alone again, not in this country. Even a trip to the privy was something a man might want to take in company. (*Collected Stories*, 450)

No walk-downs on main street or single-handed, galloping rescues on horseback here. To emphasize the cooperation needed for survival in the story, Stegner has the cowpokes tie themselves together with their lariats to help them navigate the zero visibility of the blizzard. Stumbling forward in line, with Spurlock behind him and Panguingue just ahead, Rusty finds that his

> own face was so stiff he felt he could not have spoken, even to curse, if he tried; he had lost all feeling in his lips and chin. His inhuman hook dragged at Spurlock's waist rope, he threw his shoulder across to meet Panguingue's when the weight surged too far forward, and he put foot after foot, not merely imbecilic now with cold and exhaustion, but nearly mindless. (451)

The follow-up story, "Carrion Spring," also included in *Wolf Willow* and *Collected Stories*, deals with the aftermath of that winter. The frostbitten men, although healed, are scarred, and the ranch has been put up for sale, nearly bankrupt. Two-thirds of the herd are dead and rotting on the ground all over the area. The stench is almost unbearable. The story opens with Molly Henry, wife of the foreman, her bags packed, looking around the ranch house yard for what she believes will be the last time: she and her husband are leaving. Three days of chinook has melted the snow, uncovering everything that had been under the snow since November:

> Matted, filthy, lifeless, littered, the place of her winter imprisonment was exposed, ugly enough to put gooseflesh up her backbone, and with the carrion smell over all of it. It was like a bad and disgusting wound, infected wire cut or proud flesh or the gangrene of frostbite, with the bandage off. (472)

Molly has mixed emotions. She is glad enough to be free and rid of such a place, but sorry to leave the men, who have become family to her. She looks at them, "red-bearded, black-bearded, gray-bristled . . . two of them with puckered sunken scars on the cheekbones, all of them seedy, matted-haired, weathered and cracked as old lumber left out for years," and feels a sudden desire to cry (472). It is a touching moment, her affection for this scruffy group given poignancy by her strong desire to leave. Was there ever a West less romantically described than this one?

Molly's husband, Ray, comes with the buckboard to take her to the distant town where her parents live. As they leave the ranch house behind, we are made aware of a tension between the foreman and his wife and gradually discover a complex emotional landscape. As we have just noted, she feels glad to leave the place, but sorry to leave the people; she feels sorry for her husband who so obviously feels empty and defeated and has physically suffered. And she feels guilty that it is his defeat that has allowed her to leave; yet, she looks forward to town, its comforts and female companionship. Ray, on the other hand, is glum in defeat and uncommunicative. He feels some guilt for the tough ordeal that being married to him has put her through. He is polite, but clearly unhappy and bothered by his wife's cheerfulness at leaving. They have words, and Molly says, "Oh, Ray . . . let's not crab at each other! Sure I'm glad we're getting out. Is that so awful? I hate to see you killing yourself bucking this *hopeless* country" (481).

If this is a "cowboy story" it is a very different one, one that only uses the western circumstances and surroundings to explore the complex relationship between a husband and wife. It is really a domestic story with conflicting feelings and the difficulty of expressing those feelings openly which will touch a chord in nearly all its readers, contemporary and urban as they may be. Outside, the characters are recognizable American types—the nearly silent, competent man and the effusive, loving wife; the courageous builder and the strong-willed civilizer. But it is what is going on inside that is central to the story. The conflict between the husband and wife is laid out in some detail, but at the same time universalized so as to suggest that this might well represent the terms of a conflict that might be common to any husband and wife, but particularly to those who were settling the West. Despite the fact that they see things differently, however, both husband and wife are admirable—each in his/her own way, trying hard to be considerate and thoughtful in respect to the others' needs.

What has been bothering Ray comes out eventually: he has decided that he wants to "stick," to buy the nearly ruined ranch at a bargain-basement price and run it successfully. He has said nothing about this to Molly, hoping that she would understand his needs and see the possibility for herself. Of course, after the ordeal they have just gone through nothing is further from her mind.

They stop during their journey and are sitting out on a buffalo robe eating their sandwiches when Ray tells her that "we're never goin' to have another chance like this as long as we live" (484). Molly sits, for the moment stunned by his hopes and plans, and then discovers a pale lavender crocus by her toe, a thing so unbelievable in that wretched wasteland of brown grass and frozen rivers that she exclaims with joy. That sign of life and renewal seems to signal the igniting of a small spark of hope for the future in her breast. Despite her sudden realization that in borrowing enough money to finance the purchase they would assume a burden of debt heavy enough to pin them down for life, and despite her memory of winter, "six months of unremitting slavery and imprisonment," she accedes to his wishes:

> She lifted the crocus and laid it against Ray's dark scarred cheek.
> "You should never wear lavender," she said, and giggled at the very idea, and let her eyes come up to his and stared at him, sick and scared.
> "All right," she said. "If it's what you want." (486)

Unlike Stegner's early stories, this one is not autobiographical in the strictest sense. But it does come out of his experiences in the Saskatchewan landscape and out of the values he formed while growing up with a mother he admired, who was brave and committed to her family, and a father he despised, who was footloose and who, in his search to strike it rich, pretty much ignored his wife's needs. In "Carrion Spring," the woman shows immense courage in agreeing to return to the life she has just escaped from for love of her husband. And the husband, unlike Stegner's father, was one of those that the author admired most: he is a "sticker" rather than a "boomer." A "boomer" is one who comes in, looks for an easy strike, takes what he can one way or another, and leaves; or he encounters hard times and gives up. The "stickers" are those who throughout the last century gave the West "some sort of indigenous, recognizable culture." This culture was not the product "of those who pillage and run but of those who settle, and love the life they have made and the place they have made it in" (*Bluebird*, xxii). For them, as for the foreman and his wife, western hopefulness is not a cynical joke.

Stegner's own father was the archetypal boomer in Wallace's eyes. After several years of disappointing crops on the homestead, George Stegner turned to bootlegging. And then, as Canada became increasingly wet and the U.S. passed the Volstead Act becoming dry, he looked south for opportunities. Just as earlier when the family had moved from one place to another while he looked for his main chance to make a bundle, he gave little thought to his wife and children's feelings. He wasn't disappointed or discouraged by his failure to make a fortune in Canadian wheat; instead, he was furious at being denied the wealth he thought he deserved and he was determined to leave "this dung-heeled sagebrush town on the disappearing edge of nowhere" (*Wolf Willow*, 24). As for Hilda Stegner, after five years in Saskatchewan she would be leaving the only settled home she would know during her marriage. For Wallace, those five years were the most impressionable ones of his life. He recalled years later that "I was desolate at leaving my friends, my town, my life. [On my way out of town] in the back seat I pulled a blanket over my head so that the others would not see my tears."[7]

Years later he would use this moment in a different context to end a short story, "The Colt" (1943), bringing it together with another emotional blow, the death of his colt, which had come to him the year before leaving town. The story provides a good example of how as a writer Stegner used autobiographical material, changing and combining it with fictional material. In life he had experienced a traumatic moment of horror and sadness: he had seen the colt he had loved, which had broken forelegs that he thought might heal with steel braces, skinned and rot-

23

ting on the town dump. His father had secretly arranged with a neighbor to put the animal out of its misery and the neighbor had carelessly tossed the carcass out with the garbage to rot. In the story, as the family is leaving town to go to the homestead for the summer, Bruce spots the colt with its "bloated, skinned body . . . the chestnut hair left a little way above the hooves, the iron braces still on the broken front legs" and buries his head in the blankets under him, sobbing (*Collected Stories*, 190). In thinking back on the actual discovery, Stegner has said, "I think I might eventually have accepted the colt's death, and forgiven his killer, if it had not been for that dirty little two-dollar meanness that skinned him" (*Wolf Willow*, 35).

In "The Colt" Stegner uses a device, a situational irony, that he employs frequently in his stories: building an emotional context that contrasts sharply with the emotion of the central event or revelation, using this ironic contrast to strengthen the impact of the story as a whole. Prior to his discovery of the colt's body, Bruce is seen as joyful about leaving town and optimistic about the recovery of his colt, which has been given over to the neighbor for the summer while the family is gone. There is also dramatic irony leading up to the ending, for Bruce does not know what the reader knows: that the colt has been given over to be disposed of. The more the boy exudes faith in the colt's recovery and exuberance in response to the promise of the morning, the more the reader dreads what he suspects is coming and the tension of the story builds. As the family leaves town, Bruce is in the back of the wagon singing boisterously; he jokes with his father; he even jokes about the terrible smell coming from the town dump, " 'Pee-you! Pee-you-willy!' He clamped his nose shut and pretended to fall dead" (*Collected Stories*, 189). And then the sudden discovery of the source of the smell: "He screamed at them. 'Ma, it's Socks! Stop, Pa! It's Socks!' " (189) This moment of horrified recognition is given far more weight by coming as it does out of a context of happiness and childish enthusiasm.

Leaving Eastend in 1920, George Stegner first chose to settle in Great Falls, Montana, where he ran a "blind pig," an illegal bar in his home supplied with bootlegged whiskey. Wallace recalled that

> in my first day there I made the acquaintance of things I had read about but had never seen: lawns, cement sidewalks, streetcars, streets with names, homes with numbers. . . . In the house were other things I had never seen: hardwood floors . . . a bathroom with a tub and running water, a flush toilet. (*Bluebird*, 12)

He found the whole environment wondrous but intimidating. He didn't know what he would face outside, and he was afraid of meeting strange kids on the street. By the time Wallace became somewhat adjusted to his surroundings, his father was off again to what he hoped would be greener pastures, leaving Great Falls after little more than a year to settle in Salt Lake City, where the family would stay until 1929. Wallace can remember the family living in at least 20 different houses in Salt Lake City during the years he attended junior and senior high school. His father was trying to avoid discovery by the police.

During his early teenage years, Wallace was lonely and thought of himself as a misfit. Because he had skipped two grades, he was younger and smaller than his classmates in school. There were times when he had almost no friends, and he found solace in reading and in excelling in his school work. Aside from his mother, his only source of encouragement was school, and he craved approval from his teachers. He found himself "always volunteering to do something and doing it kind of clumsily."[8] This anxiousness to please and to succeed is the basis of his story "The Volunteer" (1956), which alone among his stories deals with this painful period of his life. It is based on an experience he had during his first months in Salt Lake at South Junior High School.

"The Volunteer" is a story of self-discovery and a boy's realization that for some situations, some problems, some pain, there are no remedies. There are only rueful treaties, half-comforting gestures. The boy's feelings—his anger at his father, his irritation with his mother's sympathy, his sense of his own inadequacy—are overwhelming to him and to the reader. If we focus on the condition of the protagonist as a possible reflection of Wallace's own feelings at that time, we see a boy made to feel uncomfortable in his own home—his very presence interferes with his father's business of running a blind pig. Desperate to find some approval at school, the boy—now called David—has volunteered to make a model of a *castra*, a Roman camp, to help the class understand the Latin lessons. On the way home from school he stops to get some clay in a slough southwest of town. It is cold and he gets the wet clay all over himself while collecting it.

David arrives home wet, cold, and dirty, with a runny nose he cannot wipe clean with his muddy hands, much to the dismay of his father who is entertaining customers in the parlor. The father accuses him of making mud pies at 13, but David explains that he is supposed to make a *castra* for school: "I knew he hadn't the slightest idea what a *castra* was. . . . I knew things that he hadn't even heard of; that was a sweet

25

fierce pleasure" (*Collected Stories*, 296). David's misery is only partially relieved and his self-pity only partially dissipated by the sudden realization that his mother, who has tried to help him with his school project and who has tried to shield him from his father's anger and the dismal atmosphere of a home turned into a shabby speakeasy, has had an even more unhappy life than he. She is completely trapped, with not even the outlets of school and association with others, yet cheerfully tries to make the best of everything. His concern for her, leaving his rather constant preoccupation with his own feelings of inferiority, rejection, and self-pity, suggests an incipient maturity.

If Wallace was made tough by a harsh environment and an unforgiving and brutal father, he was toughest on himself. But he could be hard on others as well:

> Having been weak, and having hated my weakness, I am as impatient with the weakness of others as my father ever was. Pity embarrasses me for the person I am pitying, for I know how it feels to be pitied. . . . I cannot sympathize with the self-pitiers, for I have been there, or with the braggarts, for I have been there too. (*Wolf Willow*, 133)

No contemporary writer has ever been less sentimental while at the same time frequently writing about those things we are inclined to be sentimental about—love, kindness, charity, and forgiveness. Stegner has said about one of his mentors, the poet Robert Frost, that "the real jolt and force of Frost's love of life comes from the fact that it is cold at the root,"[9] and the same would seem to be true of the fiction writer.

If in life Wallace was a loner as a child and young adult, it was not by choice. He had no family life to speak of, and moving to a new location every few months made it impossible for him to make neighborhood friends. Of all things during these teenage years, he wanted most to "belong," to be an accepted part of some group. Throughout junior high, high school, and college, this yearning to belong demonstrated itself in his joining or trying to join one group after another. At first he was painfully unsuccessful. He tried to join the Boy Scouts but was too young. When he got to high school he wanted to be part of the high school ROTC, but he didn't make the minimum height and weight requirements and found himself again isolated, the only male in school without a uniform. He eventually got into the Boy Scouts, earned his merit badges, and shot up to Eagle Scout in a few months. By overeating and lifting bricks in an effort to build himself up, he was able to get into ROTC and its rifle team. And, again, by working assiduously, he rose through the ranks to first lieutenant. He wanted desperately to belong, but he was also driven to succeed—a drive that lasted a lifetime and resulted in toughness in the face of obstacles and competitiveness in nearly every activity he took up.

Several things happened to him during high school that also helped to take him out of the army of the estranged and disaffected. One was being brought into involvement with Mormon activities. He never joined the church—from his first exposure, he thought the doctrine was preposterous—but was forever grateful to the Mormons:

> I suppose one of the things that made me feel friendly to the Mormons all my life is the fact that, in Utah, again a waif and torn up again from any kind of association and friendship, somebody took me down to the Ward House one Tuesday night and here was all this going on and everybody belonging to something, you know ... So I spent all my Tuesday nights in the Ward House.[10]

There, he found dances, sports, scout meetings—friendly and welcoming people enjoying themselves. Mormon institutions were "made to order for belongers," and his attachment to the Mormons was strengthened by the many relationships, male and female, that would develop out of Ward House and school activities. His association with the Mormons would reinforce his lifelong devotion to the ideal of community and the need for cooperation, concerns that would be expressed frequently in his writing. And while he was a political liberal, there was a streak of conservative personal morality that would seem, at least in part, to have evolved out of his early Mormon associations.

Another thing that saved him was taking up tennis. Having seen him on several occasions watching tennis matches, his mother bought him a used racket. Then, on the courts he met fellow student Jack Irvine, who brought him onto the high school tennis team and subsequently became Wallace's best friend. Irvine got him a job with his father's rug company as a salesman and delivery truck driver. He also brought Wallace into his home. Irvine came from a close Mormon family, so that Wallace had a taste of normal family life for the first time.

Stegner took up the challenge of tennis like every other challenge so that by the time of graduation he was the second-ranked player on the high school team. He went on to play on the university varsity and continued with the game for much of the rest of his life. Stegner's tennis game, as well as his all-important need to find a girlfriend in high school, was helped by the fact that he shot up six inches in height early in his senior year. It was, he has said, a great gift not to be despised as a "shrimp" any longer.

One of the few times Stegner used his tennis experience in his fiction is in the short story "Balance His, Swing Yours" (1945), in which the yearning to belong and the pain of being excluded, emotions that dominated Stegner's own adolescence, are explored here, but applied to the situation of a middle-aged man, Mr. Hart. The story is one of Stegner's shorter pieces, but it is among his most complex in structure and most subtle in its implications. Hart is alone on vacation at a resort hotel in Florida; both the locale and the people are unfamiliar to him. He would like companionship and tries to take up with two young men, Tenney and Thomas, who are tanned, casual, and among the "in-group" of the resort. A fourth character, simply called the "Englishman," irritates the other characters with his pushiness, constant talk, and bragging. He is clearly "out."

Hart is careful not to be pushy and is properly dismissive of his own background and abilities. While he and the young men watch tennis it comes out that he plays, but confesses he learned at a western "cow college" and hasn't played much since. When, much to their dismay, the Englishman joins them, he begins to criticize the players on the court in a superior tone and intimates that he is a player of some prowess. Irritated and hoping to put the Englishman in his place, Hart proposes a match, and when they play, finishes him off with relish, not letting him have more than a couple of points.

On the one hand, it is clear that Hart wants acceptance from the two young men (although they remain noncommittal). On the other, there is in him throughout the story a drumbeat of irritation with the Englishman, that "dreadful little man" whom he has tried to put in his place. But Hart realizes that

> people like that would never see themselves straight. No innuendo, no humiliation, would ever teach them anything. Hopelessly inadequate, they must constantly be butting into situations and places where they don't belong. (*Collected Stories*, 67)

Although during most of the story Mr. Hart thinks that he "belongs," in a Jamesian "situation revealed" at the ending he finds that he really doesn't. At cocktail time the two young men greet him coldly and then leave him to join a group in which everyone knows everyone else and where, for the first time in his sight, they become animated. He finds himself alone, "outside the picture" (68). We see him at the end, resigned and in a sense defeated, signaling the Englishman, the only possible companion left, to join him at his table.

The complexity of the story comes in part from the ambiguous and disguised relationship of Hart to the Englishman. Stegner's use of the "center of consciousness" point of view leads us to identify and sympathize with Hart and believe, as he does, that he is being accepted, or should be, by the "in" crowd. But what the ending suggests is that the Englishman that he so thoroughly scorns acts throughout as a kind of doppelgänger, a dark twin in terms of social status, to Hart who, although he wouldn't admit it, sees himself in the Englishman's desire to impress others and fit in. That awareness, dimly, at the back of his mind, is what makes Hart so angry and so painfully aware of the Englishman's social errors. He is terribly afraid that he will be put into the same category, and this is a story of social categories.

Complexity also enters the story in a series of dichotomies that outline and emphasize the areas of belonging and not belonging in this microsociety at the resort. The two young men are casual in attitude and dress throughout; both Hart, to some extent, and the Englishman, to an exaggerated extent, are intense in their desire to belong. Hart worries a lot about what is the right thing to do under each circumstance. The young men are barefooted throughout (this is repeated over and over and becomes a symbol of their relaxed attitude, even their arrogance), whereas Hart, to some extent, and the Englishman, to a greater extent, are always depicted as somehow overdressed for each occasion.

Other dichotomies characterize belonging and not belonging. Hart is suffering from a painful and embarrassing sunburn in contrast to the young men and other resort residents who are beautifully tanned, while the Englishman, in yet another category, is seen as "fantastically white and sluglike in this garden of brown demigods" (68). Hart has gone to a western "cow college" and the Englishman implies that he is a public (private, elite) school graduate, whereas the young men don't even bother to identify their schooling but their attitude suggests a private eastern institution. The tennis that is being played as they watch earlier in the story is for Hart "Eastern tennis, the rhythmical and somehow mechanical tennis of people who learned the game as a social accomplishment" (62). He scorns it—he learned his tennis on "municipal hard courts [with] worn balls" (62)—and is certain that he could beat such players three out of four times; yet, he again misses the point. Winning is all important to him, success, whereas the lackadaisical grace of the young men suggests that such eagerness is out of place and irrelevant. When Hart plays the Englishman he does so as a kind of initiation rite that will, he believes, welcome him into the young men's sphere. His vigorous play and almost vicious desire to teach the Englishman a lesson is testimony to his eagerness to demonstrate his superiority. But Tenney and Thomas care so little they leave off watching the match long before it is over.

What we realize by reading back over the story is that Tenney and Thomas have not treated Hart with any more cordiality than they have treated the Englishman. We have been caught up in Hart's wishful thinking. Another way of stating the theme of the story is that it is a study in snobbery. All the characters are snobs in their own ways, but the snobbery of the young men—quiet, implicit, unstated—is far more powerful than Hart's sense of propriety and careful understatement, or the Englishman's more obtrusive bragging.

By the time Wallace went on to the University of Utah (his "cow college") in 1925, he no longer was driven quite so hard to belong and gain acceptance. True, he was still, at 16, the youngest of his classmates; tall and thin, a "classic stringbean," he was also a bit ill at ease both physically and socially. But he had a group of close friends he had made in tennis, and they all went on to play together for the team at the university. Although he still lived at home, he was trying to gain as much independence as possible by working at the flooring store owned by Irvine's father. As a freshman he still applied himself to his schoolwork and got "A's," but by the time he was a sophomore he had joined a fraternity and was spending much of his time with his fellow jocks, as he has called them, drinking in local beer joints, and dating heavily. He was having a very good time. Nevertheless, as a junior he recovered his academic ambition, was back on track and got mostly "A's" for the remainder of his time at Utah.

Although he had no idea he might become a writer, Stegner did consider himself "literary" and became editor of the college literary magazine. Although the university physically was a very pleasant place, there was in the background a rigid authoritarianism, a careful screening of ideas and the professors who might convey those ideas, a control that came ultimately from the watchful eye of the Mormon Church. Bright students, especially gentiles such as Stegner, often came to resent and rebel against this rigidity. His spirit of rebellion was given impetus when he encountered the writer Vardis Fisher as his freshman composition teacher. Fisher, Stegner remembered, was

> one of those teachers who like to take can openers to unopened minds. He had the notion we were all Mormon provincials, that we'd never seen anything, and that a real idea would shock the pants off us.[11]

Fisher invited him to join an informal discussion group that called itself the "Radical Club," which discussed such heretical topics as methods of birth control and the historicity of Jesus Christ. An indication of the mixed emotions that Wallace had toward his professor is revealed in his ambivalent treatment of the character Paul Latour in "The View from the Balcony," a story that takes its setting out of Stegner's graduate school years and that we will look at in the next chapter.

Stories Related to the College Years

During Wallace's last two years at the University of Utah, 1928 to 1930, a woman friend by the name of Peg Foster took over the shepherding of his rebellion where Fisher left off. Attractive, in her early 20s, and living off-campus in an apartment, Foster ran a literary salon for the brighter young professors of English literature and their most promising students. Wallace recalls that despite the airless quality of the university,

> I don't think we all felt starved for culture. I don't think we had any capacity for culture. That's where . . . Peg Foster came in because she wrote poetry and she knew a lot of poetry. It was kind of nice, off the university grounds as it were, to run into somebody who took poetry seriously. (Stegner, Interview, July 20, 1987)

A close friend of Wallace, Red Cowan, who was on the tennis team and also worked at the flooring store, remembers Foster as a "rather exotic creature" with slinky dresses, figured shawls, and dangling earrings. Like members of the Radical Club, Peg Foster's group loved to poke fun at what it considered narrow-minded, bourgeois Salt Lake.

One of a series of stories that deals with Stegner's late college years, "Maiden in a Tower" (1954) features a character modeled after Foster. Just as in his novel *Recapitulation*, "Maiden in a Tower," is told in retrospect, by an older man whose memory has been jogged by returning to Salt Lake. Again, as in "Balance His, Swing Yours," we have a story with an undertow but whereas in the tennis story it is the pain of not belonging here it is the pain of regret for the failure to act.

Kimball Harris is the man who takes a journey in memory, back 25 years to a Bohemian life in the salon of the beautiful Holly. The journey starts in the present when he returns to Salt Lake in order to make arrangements for the burial of what was his last living close relative, Aunt Margaret, "never very lovable, never dear to him" (*Collected Stories*, 271). Already as Kimball drives into the city he finds himself "alert with the odd notion that he was returning both through distance and through time" (268). When he looks up the address of the funeral parlor in the phone book, he is almost certain that it is located in the very house where Holly's apartment had been and the memories began to flood back:

> Painters of bile-green landscapes, makers of cherished prose, dream-tellers, correspondence-school psychoanalysts, they had swarmed through Holly's apartment and eddied around her queenly shape with noises like breaking china. He remembered her in her gold gown, a Proserpine or Circe. For an instant she was slim and tall in his mind and he saw her laughing in the midst of the excitement she created, and how her hair was smooth black and her eyes very dark blue and how she wore massive gold hoops in her ears. (269)

After going to the address and recognizing the house with its three-story stone tower, he is greeted by the mortician and they conclude the burial arrangements. On impulse he asks if he might see what had been Holly's third floor apartment; he is given permission but warned that there is a woman's body there, dressed, but laid out in preparation for burial. The woman is a stranger but the room, almost empty, is dominated by her presence. A Navajo squash-blossom necklace stands out in almost shocking contrast to her nondescript appearance and simple black dress. She becomes for Harris a talisman, not so much for specific memories as for his emotions in response to all that comes back to him. The bright, blooming necklace against the dark dress seems to suggest a giving-over to the joy of life: "What it said of frivolity, girlishness, love of ornament and of gaiety and of life made him like her," but "the way it lay on the sober black crepe breast preached the saddest lesson he had ever learned" (278).

What that lesson might be is not given to us explicitly. But what we do know from the story is that at a crucial moment in his past Kimball failed to embrace life, failed to take the risk. Holly was not only beautiful, provocative, the center of attention, the girl every man around her was in love with, but she was a risk-taker, a generator of excitement. Typical was her plan for the miniature golf course across the street: she would fill the water holes with crocodiles, sow the sandtraps with sidewinders, and "hide a black widow spider in every hole so that holing out and picking up your ball would earn you some excitement" (274). Harris remembers, "Live it dangerously. It was strange to recall how essential that had seemed" (274).

However, there was a play-acting quality to the salon, everyone taking on a Bohemian-prescribed role in reaction to the safe, sane—and dull—

surroundings of the Mormon city. In retrospect, Harris realizes that "under the sheath [Holly] was positively virginal; if you cracked the enamel of her sophistication you found a delighted little girl playing life" (275). Their relationship had been a flirtatious game, so ingrained in him that one day near the end of Holly's reign in the apartment, when life suddenly becomes real, he is unable to respond to the challenge, unable "to live dangerously." Pressing against Harris and crying, Holly had begged him, "Kim, Kim, get me out of here! I want to get out of this. This is all no good, I've got to, Kim, please!" (276)

But Harris had played the game of make-believe emotion too long and retreated into mock consolation, patting her on the head. He finds the memory of this moment of immaturity and timidity humiliating. Although from "a life of prudence" he has gotten a wife and children he cares for deeply, it seems to him, as he stands there in that room in the mortuary remembering Holly, that "his failure to take her when she offered herself was one of the saddest failures of his life" (277). It is a memory that he has repressed, and coming back under these circumstances fills him with regret. Or, to frame the moment in terms of the Robert Frost poem, it was a place where the road divided and he took the one most traveled, the one most comfortable. As Harris leaves the room and the dead body within, he hears, almost in panic, "the four quick raps his heels made on the bare floor before they found the consoling softness of the stairs" (278)—perhaps he has heard "Time's winged chariot," or maybe it is the person he used to be, dogging his heels.

The story is an investigation into safety and risk, life and death, ongoing experience and memory. It emphasizes the importance of the quality of life, the need to embrace life totally and take the chance. As in so much of Stegner's fiction, especially his later work, the past and present are woven together to become all of one piece, so that the present derives its meaning from the past and the past defines our identity. We see this use of time in several of the stories, but more obviously in novels such as *Recapitulation*, *Angle of Repose*, and *Crossing to Safety*. Stegner made a conscious effort in his fiction to, in his words, "interpenetrate the past and present," and in several places stated his goal was to do for the West what Faulkner had done for Mississippi, discover "a usable continuity between the past and present."[12] Of course, it was an effort that demonstrated itself in much of his fiction whether it was set in the West or not.

Another of the stories that intermixes memories with present experience and like "Maiden in a Tower" goes back in its recollections to the central character's college days is "Beyond the Glass Mountain" (1947). While both pieces are about memory, its place in this story is not so much about regret for actions not taken, as about nostalgia—the sentimentalizing of the past, which is then seen to be in conflict with reality. We are also involved here with the conflicting perspectives of different times and different people. Do people change so much over time that we can no longer reach them? Can we ever really say that we know another person? Understand their situation? The main character, Mark Aker, has become an Easterner, is a success, a well-known and well-traveled scientist. In a trip back to his undergraduate university (Iowa, where Stegner went to graduate school), like Kimball Harris in the previous story he finds himself trying to recover the feelings of his past:

> Odd compulsions moved him. He found himself reciting the names of all the main university buildings. . . . Mark looked curiously at the few students he met, wondering if they felt as he felt the charm and warmth that lay in the brick streets and the sleepy river and the sun-warmed brick and stone of the university. . . . All of it was still there—unimaginably varied smells and sounds and sights that together made up the way he had once lived, the thing he had once been, perhaps the thing he still was. (*Collected Stories*, 23–24)

But just as in "Balance His, Swing Yours," Stegner sets up the reader for a reversal through his use of the center-of-consciousness point of view. We are led to identify with Mark Aker—a straight-shooter who only wants to be helpful—to share his warm response to the past, but most of all to share his expectations in regard to renewing his friendship with his old roommate, Mel. Then Stegner sets out to undermine that warm feeling and those expectations by dropping bits and pieces of information that first plant a seed of unease in our minds and then make it grow until it becomes distress.

Mark is grateful to Mel for all he did for him during their undergraduate days. He had looked up to Mel as a model, a gracious, sharing person who taught their whole group some important values. But as Mark went on to success, Mel was left behind in a bad marriage and confining job in Iowa City. In college Mel put on a drunk act which, along with calling Mark "Canby" (for some unknown reason), became a running joke between them. Over the years Mel's drunk act made it impossible for Mark to communicate anything directly to him over the telephone. But Mark felt that behind the act Mel was reaching out for help of some kind. Now, on his return to Iowa City, Mark calls Mel on the phone and

35

is baffled when Mel takes up his routine again and goes on and on with it. Is he simply taking the joke too far or has he become permanently a drunk, a caricature of himself?

At Mel's house Mark renews acquaintance with Mel's wife, Tamsen, who "had always been shrewd, and . . . had been all her life one of the world's most accomplished liars" (27). In college she had slept around and more recently she and Mel nearly divorced as a result of her affair with a golf pro. Now she seems to encourage her husband's drinking. As Mark's visit continues, it becomes clear that the underlying atmosphere of the house is poisonous, while on the surface they keep up the charade of a jovial reunion. Late in the story, Mark can only tell Mel what he wants to tell him in his mind:

> For the love of God, get that divorce, for the sake of the boy and for your own sake. She'll suck you dry, like an old orange skin. You're already so far gone I could cry—soggy with alcohol and with that comedy-routine front on all the time. Come and stay with me, I'll line you up with Alcoholics Anonymous if you want. Give me a chance to pay some of what I owe you. (28)

But, he realizes, "You simply did not say things like that" (28).

At the end of his visit Mark makes one last, lame attempt to break through his friend's defenses, gripping his hand and looking into his eyes, telling him that he wishes him the best and starts to offer, in general terms, his help. But

> he stopped. Mel was looking at him without any of the sodden fuzziness that had marked him for the past hour. His eyes were pained, intent, sad. On his delicate bruised lips there was a flicker of derision. (31)

In those last words, "a flicker of derision," the story seems to deconstruct and fall to pieces at the bottom of our minds. What are we to make of this? Right before this ending, as the two men take leave of Tamsen at the door (Mel will walk Mark to the corner), Mark is "trying to decide whether the look in her clear eyes had been triumphant, or whether there had actually been any look at all" (30). The sense one gets from this and other tidbits about Tamsen's influence on her husband is that she seems to be operating more or less as the evil corrupter and has been during Mark's visit in combat with him, the "rescuing angel," for Mel's soul. Does Mel's expression, the "flicker of derision" indicate that he is irretrievably lost, or that he is not lost at all but playing a game with everyone including his wife, or simply that he scorns what he perceives as Mark's superior attitude, his condescension, his pity? Has Mark's earlier relationship with Mel blinded him to his friend's real situation, or have his values, his successes blinded him to his friend's chosen values and needs?

We can go back to a Stegner story about childhood, such as "Two Rivers," and see some of the same questions being raised. Can two people really know each other—even a son and his mother? How do our past and memories of the past, with differing reactions to the same events, influence our present identities?

One other story that brings together time, identity, and communication—or lack of it—and is set in the period of Stegner's graduate school years, "The Blue-Winged Teal" (1950), is one of Stegner's best known pieces. It, too, ends in a "situation revealed" revealed in puzzling ambiguity, raising more questions than it answers. As much as any other short fiction that Stegner ever wrote, this is a story of atmosphere—an atmosphere that is dreary, shabby, and charged with barely suppressed hostility and despair. The story's setting, time and place, is patterned on a very traumatic period in Stegner's own life. After graduating from the University of Utah (in 1930) and going on to graduate school at the University of Iowa for two years, he was staying with his father in an apartment in Salt Lake City. His mother had just suffered a terrible death from cancer, and when her pain had become too severe, his father had fled the scene, leaving Wallace to care for his mother until her death. Wallace never forgave his father and had come to hate him, not only for abandoning his wife during her crisis, but for the outlaw pattern of living over the years that had isolated her and deprived the family of any kind of normal existence. While Wallace had been in graduate school, the banks had failed, taking all his savings, and having left school to take care of his mother, he was now stuck with and dependent on his father until a new semester started and he could resume his studies. It was a bitter pill to swallow.

While the superficial circumstances are changed and the events and supporting characters are imagined in the story, the central emotion, the son's hatred for his father, remains, patterned after the author's actual feelings. One might guess that "The Blue-Winged Teal" was, among other things, an exorcism of emotions that Stegner had struggled with for much of his life. The dominant scene in the story is a poolroom that is managed by the father. In life Stegner's own father was between occupations, having sold his interest in a Reno gambling house. In the story father and son share a single furnished room, making the situation for the son even more claustrophobic and unbearable.

Although the son is called Henry here, one could think of this as the last of the "Bruce stories," the stories based on Stegner's growing up. (Indeed, as the story appears in the novel *Recapitulation* the son's name is Bruce and the father's name is George Mason rather than John Lederer, as he is called in the story.) "The Blue-Winged Teal" can be seen to serve as a coda to the father-son relationship at the heart of these stories. The son, now an adult, reflects back on the relationship and in an epiphany near the end of the story he finds himself having the disturbing suspicion that there may well be another side to the story of his father and that in judging his father so severely he may have been at least in part mistaken.

At loose ends, and at odds with his father and the world, Henry has, on an impulse he doesn't understand, borrowed his father's shotgun, waders, and car and has gone duck hunting. Standing in front of his father's pool hall and loaded down with nine ducks, he wonders whatever possessed him to go. In the description that follows, Stegner reverses that sense of space and naturalness in prairie or woods he uses so often in other stories to define the condition of his protagonist. Henry's emotional condition, depressed and antagonistic, is revealed in the dark, enclosed, and shabby scene he anticipates he will encounter after descending the stairs from the street down into his father's pool hall:

> He would find, sour contrast with the bright sky and the wind of the tulle marshes, the cavelike room with its back corners in darkness, would smell that smell compounded of steam heat and cue-chalk dust, of sodden butts in cuspidors, of coffee and meat and beer smells from the counter, of cigarette smoke so unaired that it darkened the walls. From anywhere back of the middle tables there would be the pervasive reek of toilet disinfectant. (232)

After entering, Henry slides the string of ducks off his shoulder and swings them over onto the bar: "They landed solidly—offering or tribute or ransom or whatever they were" (233).

The story goes on to trace the emotional swings of Henry's relationship to his father. Like a man in prison—and he feels as if he is—whose mood may alternate between despair and hope, Henry's attitude toward his father alternates between hatred and disgust on the one hand and a reluctant movement toward some slight sympathy on the other. What really sticks in his craw, however, is his father's easy return to his old pattern of illegal activities before he was married (managing an establishment that provides gambling and drinking) and, especially, his taking up with the red-haired woman who comes into the pool hall late at night waiting for him to close up. Henry considers her an insult to his mother's memory.

The father is pleased that there are enough ducks to give them a "real old-fashioned feed" (235), and that, in turn, reminds him of good times in the past that he and his son have shared. But Henry is determined to hold on to his hatred and not be drawn into his father's nostalgia. He refuses to let the moment ease the strain that has been between them: "He did not forgive his father the poolhall, or [was he willing to] forget the way the old man had sprung back into the old pattern, as if his wife had been a jailer and he was now released" (235).

A climax to the story comes that night as Henry lies in bed in the furnished room, awakened by his father coming home late and undressing in the dark. While pretending to be asleep, Henry smells

> the smells his father brought with him: wet wool, stale tobacco, liquor; and above all, more penetrating than any, spreading through the room and polluting everything there, the echo of cheap musky perfume. (237)

The perfume drives him to rage at himself for the sympathy, as slight as it was, that he had felt for his father earlier in the day.

In a reversal of Nick Adams's systematic procedure to keep himself awake in Hemingway's "Now I Lay Me," carefully fishing in his mind every hole in a remembered stream, Henry is able to block out his anger and lead himself into sleep by bringing into his mind a lit pool table. It is a deliberate, almost too obvious irony, yet it works well to suggest Henry's internal battle to take control of his mind and to suppress his rage in response to the perfume. Mentally, he carefully racks up the balls, breaks them, and one after another lines up each shot and pockets the balls. He knows that eventually "nothing would remain in his mind but the *clean* green cloth traced with running color and bounded by *simple* problems" [my emphasis] and that sometime in the middle of an intricate shot, he will slide off into sleep (241). That is to say, "If only life could be so simple; if only we had such control over our lives when we are awake."

But Henry's feelings shift yet again. The next day his anger leads him to find the old friends that, for some reason he cannot fathom, he has been avoiding and borrow enough money to break out of his paralysis, get to the coast, and renew his life. He has been deliberately nursing his hatred, bringing to mind those things that might most stimulate his anger, but now he seems willing to let go. With a sense of release, he returns to the pool hall to tell his father he is leaving, only to find that he had forgotten about the duck feed. During dinner at the counter in the pool hall, once again his father reflects on times gone by, and when he recalls the mother's hand-painted china, his son responds by sitting "stiffly, angry that his mother's name should even be mentioned between them in this murky hole" (244).

His father has taken duck wings and tacked them up on the mirror frame behind the bar: " 'Blue-wing teal,' his father said ... 'Just the wings, like that. Awful pretty. She thought a teal was about the prettiest little duck there was' " (244). The teal and their feathers are seen in the story as soft, gentle, and beautiful—their fragility and beauty a reminder of a soft and loving woman who is gone and a family that has been broken. Pinned up on the wall, they become an emblem of what was tender between the father and mother that their son will never take part in. Self-centered in his own mourning, Henry focuses almost exclusively on his own feelings, not even recognizing the possibility that his father, in his own way, may have cared deeply about his mother.

After talking about his wife and how she responded to the beauty of the teal, Henry's father suddenly breaks apart. His eyes fill with tears and he stumbles down the stairs and through the pool tables to the toilet in the back. His son, shocked by his father's anguished look before he ran, thinks:

> The hell with you, the look had said. The hell with you ... my son Henry. The hell with your ignorance, whether you're stupid or whether you just don't know all you think you know. You don't know enough to kick dirt down a hole. You know nothing at all, you know less than nothing because you know things wrong. (245)

This moment of revelation tears away the foundation of the son's anger, leaving him empty, somewhat bewildered, and wondering "if there was anything more to his life, or his father's life, ... or anyone's life, than playing the careful games that deadened you into sleep" (246).

Later, after returning to his counter, Henry's father starts to clean up the dishes from their dinner. His son takes that moment to say what he has come to say—telling his father that he will be leaving town:

> But he did not say it in anger, or with the cold command of himself that he had imagined in advance. He said it like a cry, and with the feeling he might have had on letting go the hand of a friend too weak and too exhausted to cling any longer to their inadequate shared driftwood in a wide cold sea. (246)

This ambiguous metaphor that finishes the story has, like so many Stegner endings, multiple suggestive meanings. One such, certainly, is that the son realizes that despite his father's seedy life he did love his wife and the three of them did have a family, regardless of its flaws. Without the mother, the warm, loving center of their lives, they are now both cast adrift on the cold sea of life. And further, Henry seems to realize that of the two of them, he and his father, he is the strongest, least dependent, and best able to make a life for himself. But still clinging to his driftwood on a frigid and barren sea, his life would seem to hold minimal promise—but he will survive, while his father is clearly lost.

This step toward forgiveness was not taken in life by Stegner until old age, when his anger dissipated and sorrow took its place, long after his father took his own life. The fiction provides an occasion for insight and forgiveness that life did not. What may strike us most about "The Blue-Winged Teal" is how, once again, the field has been reversed: how we are seduced by the son's emotions surrounding his father, which seem so justified until we and the son discover how mistaken we are. The lesson seems to be how easily we are led to be judgmental, lacking charity, lacking empathy, and lacking insight into the emotional conditions of others. The path of Henry's emotions is even more complex than summarized here. The story is a masterpiece of counterpoint, overtone, suggestive imagery, and skillful employment of point of view.

After returning to graduate school at the University of Iowa in 1934, accompanied by his longtime friend Red Cowan, Stegner found his circumstances changed in several ways. He had obtained his master's by writing three short stories for his thesis, but his graduate advisor, Norman Foerster, suggested to him that he would have a hard time getting a college teaching job with an M.A. in creative writing and advised him to pursue a Ph.D. in American literature. Wallace found himself in a highly structured and very demanding academic program, feeling totally inadequate to the task. Through the good offices of his former graduate school roommate, Wilbur Schramm, he was able to find a temporary job teaching four classes at half-time pay at a small Lutheran school, Augustana College, in Rock Island, Illinois. On Thursday evenings after classes were over, he would hitchhike the 50 miles to Iowa City, where he studied for his doctoral exams over the weekend.

Wilbur Schramm also introduced Wallace to his future wife, Mary Page. A graduate student in English who worked in the university library at Iowa, Mary was delighted to go out on a blind date with Wilbur's friend. She had read the stories that Wallace had written for his master's degree and was impressed by them. She was very attractive—pixie-like, so small and young looking that on at least one occasion she was mistaken for Wallace's daughter when they were together. Because she was well-read and intellectual, she and Wallace had a great deal in common, and he fell deeply in love with her. During the three-day weekends Wallace had at the university, they spent as much time together as he could spare from his studies, and usually, since he had very little money, they spent their time just walking and talking. During the week while he was at Augustana, he wrote letter after letter to her, even though his letters might arrive in Iowa City after he did.

In the meantime Wallace's old friend Red Cowan had found a place to live near the university with a group of graduate students who had taken over an abandoned fraternity house. Cowan recalls that it was "a great place to party," and Wallace and Mary were usually invited. It was this house and these Saturday night graduate student bashes that became the models for the setting and occasion for Wallace's story, written long afterward, "The View from the Balcony" (1948). The larger setting, however, is moved from the University of Iowa to the University of Indiana (possibly because Stegner had no connection at all to Indiana). Another ingredient that came into the story more contemporaneously with its composition was Wallace's experiences in teaching World War II veterans. Since in the postwar period he was very close in age to these veterans, he came to know them on a more personal basis, their families and problems, than students he encountered before or after.

Back in his own graduate days, Wallace, along with Mary, gradually became disenchanted with the Red Cowan crowd. Cowan recalls that another mutual friend, Don Lewis, invited Vardis Fisher and his wife out from Idaho, and they stayed in the fraternity house:

Fisher immediately dubbed it Eagle Heights [the house in the story is on a hill overlooking a park and river]. He was a heavy drinker, a loud, violent man and very caustic in his comments about everybody. All of this proved too much for Mary. She didn't like it, so Wally and Mary didn't associate very much with the crowd.[13]

Fisher, who had been Stegner's writing instructor at Utah, had by this time published a book of poetry and several novels (over his career he would publish some 30 books, the best known being the novel *Children of God: An American Epic* [1939]). The obnoxious Fisher would become the model for Paul Latour in "The View from the Balcony"—not the main character but the catalyst for the action, something close to a villain.

"The View from the Balcony" takes up a theme common to much of Stegner's fiction—the unfeeling and irresistible power of nature, expressed most vividly here in a pattern of animal imagery. We see this power expressed not only in the natural surroundings, but in human nature as well, and it makes us uneasy by underlining our fundamental insecurity. In the story a group of graduate students are having a celebratory party on the roof terrace of their rooming house for one of the group who will, by the time of the party, have taken and presumably passed his Ph.D. exam. However, the party takes a grim direction, first, when it is learned that the student, filled with dread, walked out of the exam without taking it, and, second, when one of the guests, a psychology professor, in the heat of the party's activity challenges and actually physically wrestles one of his advisees, Charley Graham, and at one point nearly throws him off the roof.

The professor, Paul Latour, is described as having "a face . . . like the face of a predatory bird, beaked, grim lipped" (96), and the wrestling match takes on the air of some sort of animal ritual in which the older Latour is defending his leadership of the pack against a younger challenger (not too far off the mark in expressing in physical terms the atmosphere in some university departments). Latour tells Charley, "Given half a chance . . . you'd open your wolfish jaws and swallow me, You're like the cannibals who think it gives them virtue to eat their enemy's heart. You'd eat mine" (99). The contest, which begins as a sort of rugged party game, gradually escalates to a real life-and-death struggle. Charley's wife stands by appalled by the spectacle.

Later, sexuality, with animal-like overtones, comes to the fore when another professor has his wife willingly carried off during the party by

43

one of the students into the "jungle," the brush and trees surrounding the river below the terrace. These and other incidents emphasize the irrational, the animalistic, the primitive that really seem to drive these people in what might normally be thought of as the intellectual and refined atmosphere of the graduate school. Indeed, a veneer of civilized normality stands in ironic contrast to the episodes of the primitive in the story. The events take place on the campus of a university in the bosom of American ordinariness, the Midwest—an odd place to find a "jungle" complete with animal sounds—and Charley Graham seems to be your typical all-American nice young man, but he reveals a determination, "killer-instinct" that Tommy Probst, the graduate student who abandoned his exam, lacks. Latour may not have been so wrong in his assessment of Charley after all.

Below the terrace on the other side of the river is the city zoo, and roars from the lions penetrate the darkness during the party, punctuating the ongoing displays of primitive human emotion. The roars are particularly chilling to Charley's British war bride, Lucy, who during the course of the story becomes increasingly emotionally isolated from these ex-GI's who are, with one exception, so smug in themselves and confident of the future. When the party breaks up, there is a search for the missing wife of the faculty member, and for an instant as Lucy looks out from the roof into the darkness below, she sees, in the flash of headlights from a car, a canoe on the river with a couple in it.

A moment later she finds it hard to believe that she saw what she saw. She even feels

> a little knife-prick of terror that it could have been there—so silent, so secret, so swallowed in the black, as unseen and unfelt and unsuspected as a crocodile at a jungle ford. (104)

Heat lightning flares and she holds her breath waiting for the sound of thunder, but none comes. Instead, at that instant, the lion chooses to roar again. Her heart pounds as she thinks,

> What if he should be loose?
> What if, in these Indiana woods by this quiet river where all of them lived and worked for a future full of casual expectation, far from the jungles and the veldts where lions could be expected and where darkness was full of danger, what if here too fear prowled on quiet pads and made its snarling noise in the night? (104)

Her epiphany brings her to a realization that their sense of "normality" and their common assumptions and hopes are "as friable as walls of cane" (105). She realizes that she and her friends, in their hearts, are actually "alone, terrified, and at bay, each with his ears attuned to some roar across the woods, some ripple of the water, some whisper of a footstep in the dark" (105).

Fear prowls on quiet pads throughout the world, whether in Africa or the American Midwest, for it is not just the lion that can bring it, but the potential for violence in every human breast. We humans tend to circle the wagons and light the campfire to frighten away the wolves or bears or mountain lions, but what if the real danger is already inside the circle? Inside our husband or wife? Inside ourselves? The challenge of the Ph.D. exam and the fear it inspires, the Paul Latour wrestling match where the advisor turns viciously on his advisee, the missing faculty wife who abandons her husband, and the roar of the lion all suggest that there is no such thing as safety, security, or predictability in life. At the same time these external events signify the dangers that at any moment can unpredictably assault us from the vagaries of human emotion. The story is about fate and fear, and every one of the events touches Lucy in some way: the threat to her husband's professional future, the killer-instinct that her husband suddenly displays, and the friability of marriage as suggested by the missing wife. We shall see this theme of fate, fear, and human vulnerability in other Stegner stories.

The Influence of Robert Frost and Stories Set in Vermont

At the time that Stegner was finishing his Ph.D., he and Mary Page decided to get married. The ceremony, in the presence of a few family friends, was performed at Mary's home in Dubuque, and shortly after the wedding the two of them drove in Wallace's old Model A to Salt Lake City. There, he had obtained a job as an instructor of English for $1,700 a year at his alma mater, the University of Utah.

Exhausted from finishing his dissertation, he was glad to be able to relax a bit, settling into his full-time teaching job at a school where he felt very much at home and where he had many friends. The newly married couple found time to enjoy themselves, socializing with other young staff members and their spouses and on weekends taking picnic lunches up into the canyons above the city where Wallace had hiked as a teenager. There was only one catch to their happiness—they had a very difficult time making ends meet, and while they were overjoyed that Mary was pregnant, they were concerned about being able to afford a new member of the family. Wallace was worried enough to go back to work on a temporary basis at the flooring store in Salt Lake during school vacation periods.

It was in large part this concern for money that prompted him to write what would become his first significant publication, the short novel *Remembering Laughter* (1937). Although he had written short stories as an undergraduate and had used three stories for his master's thesis, he still had no idea of becoming a writer, no idea, as he has said, that "one *could* become a writer." Nevertheless, while reading a magazine one day in the fall of 1936, he spotted an advertisement that announced a $2,500 prize offered by the well-known publisher, Little, Brown and Company, for the best novelette manuscript. He thought, "I can do that—I can write a novelette," and perhaps he would win and their money problems would be solved. It was almost an act of desperation. His first major publication would not come out of lofty literary ambition or the impulse of sudden artistic inspiration.

The writing took him only three hours a day, spent before he went on campus for his classes. The writing went easily and in six weeks he was finished. "I don't remember having the slightest trouble with it." He sent in the manuscript and more or less forgot about it. Then, months later, on January 30, 1937 as they were lying in bed in their Salt Lake City apartment, the Stegners were awakened in the middle of the night with a telegram. They had won the prize—they were rich! Wallace recalled:

> We had a party, quite a party. At the end, Mary went into labor, and after a couple of hard days produced a son. My new family responsibilities and my new literary life began together.[14]

The story he wrote was almost ready-made, based on something Mary had told him about a scandal among distant relations having to do with adultery between a husband and his wife's sister. Of course, content is one thing, but the manner of the story's telling, was quite another, and it was his artistic skill, which would seem to have come out of raw talent rather than experience, that made the novelette a work of fiction beyond the ordinary. For one thing, he employed a relatively sophisticated narrative method, withholding information which created suspense, leading the reader to wonder why the relations in this family were so strained. Then the mystery is resolved gradually through a carefully constructed series of flashbacks. For another, he employed description of farm life and natural surroundings so vivid and believable that many readers wrote to him to say that they found the novelette very moving, evoking memories of childhood experiences on their family farm in Iowa (or Illinois or Wisconsin).

The importance of *Remembering Laughter* for Stegner's career was that it did, indeed, begin his "literary life." More important, the prize assured him of something that he hadn't really considered seriously—that he could become a writer. Beyond that, it gave him a small measure of celebrity, providing a platform for later achievement and making it easier for him to publish, as well as putting a star on his résumé as he applied for teaching jobs. Without the prize not only might he have abandoned his writing career before it even started, but his life would have certainly taken a far different course.

Remembering Laughter was the only novelette he ever wrote, although two of his short stories are nearly long enough to qualify: "Genesis" (74 pages) and "A Field Guide to the Western Birds" (48 pages). The short story and the novel were his forms. If a story began to extend itself, he was usually tempted to turn it into a full-length novel. He thought "Genesis" (1959) would be a novel, but decided to cut it off when he began to wonder where it was going. He decided to make "Field Guide to the Western Birds" (1956) into a novel (combining it with an unpublished story, "Indoor-Outdoor Living"), but the resulting novel, *All the Little Live Things*, while using some of the same characters in the same setting, tells a very different story than either of its predecessors.

Stegner went on from his prize-winning novelette to a career as a writer of both short stories and novels, although he achieved more success, early on, with his stories. As a story writer he had two bursts of activity: from 1938 to 1943, when he published 18 stories, and from 1947 to 1958, when he published 15. It wasn't until 1943, several years after he had made his mark as a story writer, that he had his first success with a full-length novel, *The Big Rock Candy Mountain*, which, by the way, incorporated several of his early stories about growing up in Saskatchewan. With the exception of "The Women on the Wall" (1946), there was a hiatus for the last two years of the war and the year after while he was working as a reporter and changing teaching jobs. By the mid-1950s he had become known as a major practitioner of the short story form. His work appeared in several well-regarded, large-circulation magazines, and many stories were republished in general anthologies as well as in collections aimed at schools and colleges. Certifying his status was a string of years in which his stories were included in the annual *Best American Short Stories* and the *O. Henry Memorial Award Prize Stories*. 1950 saw the publication of the first collection entirely devoted to his own stories, *The Women on the Wall*, and 1956, the second, *The City of the Living*.

What characterized his short fiction was that it had very little overt action, but depended, as we have seen, on evolving psychological states—perceptions of oneself and others, situations or environments that generate emotions and quiet realizations. In the quiet, slowly developing power of his stories we can see the influence of the writer he admired most, Anton Chekhov: "The world," Stegner once said to a colleague, "is divided into those for whom Tolstoy is the greatest or Anton Chekhov, and short story writers always prefer Chekhov."[15] On another occasion, explaining what he had learned from the Russian writer, he said, "Chekhov had a way of turning up the rheostat, little by little . . . Joyce called it an epiphany. Katherine Mansfield called it a nuance."[16]

Two other writers Stegner expressed particular admiration for were Joseph Conrad, the first major literary figure whose work he had read as a youngster, and William Faulkner. Conrad provided example to him, through his use of the narrator Marlowe, of the importance of point of view, an importance Stegner stressed over and over again to his creative writing students. Faulkner reinforced Stegner's own sense of the importance of history and led him to his own frequent experiments with the manipulation of time in his fiction: Faulkner had taught him that in literature one can represent the past and the present as all of one piece. We can see this bringing together of past and present in several of Stegner's stories, including two that we will be looking at shortly, "The Sweetness of the Twisted Apples" and "The Traveler." We have already seen it in "Two Rivers," "Maiden in a Tower," "The Blue-Winged Teal," and "Beyond the Glass Mountain."

Because of his familiarity with the work of nearly all the major short story writers of times past, as well as of his own time (he also would come to know many of them personally and invite them to lecture or teach in his creative writing program), and after extensive experience of teaching short story writing, Wallace would develop a very flexible, inclusive view of the form. Late in life, at a reading on his book tour to publicize the publication of his *Collected Stories* (1990), he said,

> I don't have any formula or theory of the short story. The only thing I do demand of a short story, my own or anyone else's, is that it ought to close some sort of circuit—a plot circuit, an emotional circuit, psychological circuit, a circuit of understanding, so in the end there is some sense of completion. (Kazak, 29)

Having won the novelette prize and some status as a writer, Stegner felt that he should be able to leave the ranks of instructor, a temporary, low-paying position, to be hired by the University of Utah as a tenure-track, assistant professor. However, no one had been hired on tenure-track for years, and even after he made personal application to the university's president, he was refused, told that the school simply could not afford permanent hiring in the midst of the Depression. With the prize money Stegner had no immediate money worries, but looking ahead, with not only a wife but a new baby to support, he felt he would have to have a better salary and more security.

After rewarding themselves by taking part of their money for a bicycle tour of England and France, the Stegners went on to Madison, where Wallace had taken a job at the University of Wisconsin as an assistant professor. Two things happened during his years at Wisconsin that profoundly influenced both his life and the direction of his short stories. The first was meeting Phil and Peg Gray. Phil was another young professor at the university and he and his wife had come out of a background of eastern wealth and privilege—quite different from that of the Stegners. Nevertheless they embraced the westerners warmly, becoming close friends, a friendship that lasted decades and was so meaningful to the Stegners that Wallace made it the subject of his last novel, *Crossing to Safety*, written after Phil and Peg Gray's death.

The Grays introduced the Stegners to Vermont, which would become the setting for several of Wallace's short stories. The Gray family had a vacation compound on the shore of Caspian Lake, near the village of Greensboro. The Stegners stayed with the Grays in their large summer home during the summer of 1938 and liked the area so much that they bought an old farm with a dilapidated house that they began to restore that very summer. In the meantime, the second important that thing happened to Wallace while he was at Wisconsin was an invitation in 1938 to teach at Bread Loaf, the granddaddy of summer writing conferences, which was also in Vermont. He would teach or lecture there for almost a decade, and it was there he met, among other celebrities, Robert Frost and Bernard DeVoto. Both would befriend the young writer and mentor him.

Despite the fact that on the property they had purchased the barn was destroyed and the house badly damaged by a hurricane in the winter of 1938–1939, the Stegners were in the area to stay, returning nearly every summer for the rest of their lives. Certainly the presence of the Grays increased the area's attraction, but also Wallace's encounters with Frost at Bread Loaf, the author of all those Vermont poems that Stegner had taught and knew so well, gave the country for him a special glow. At graduate school at the University of Iowa, Stegner had been immersed in Americana and by his graduate advisor, Norman Foerster, was convinced of the importance for writers to explore all that was native to the American experience, and certainly there was nothing more "Americana" than Robert Frost's New England. Frost himself, Stegner has said, was "as much in the American grain as Lincoln or Thoreau."[17]

Looking closely at the stories and novels Stegner wrote about Vermont, it becomes apparent that it was difficult for him even to think about the area without Frost's language and themes coming to mind. Beyond that, although we may think of Stegner as essentially a Western writer, what he found in Vermont seems to have taken the place of a West that was disappearing, or perhaps a West that never was. Here was a part of the country that was uncrowded, with room to walk and roam, with trees—there was so much moisture that you couldn't stop the trees and brush from growing, from replacing themselves rapidly when they had been cut back. It was also a place that displayed the best of Western virtues, a spirit of community and strong connection to the land. In speaking of Greensboro, Stegner said,

> Everybody grows up working hard, and at all kinds of jobs. They're jacks-of-all-trades. They can fix things, toggle them up. That's characteristic of any frontier, and that's the kind of West that I grew up in.[18]

Tying together with these evaluative responses to the Vermont setting was Frost's reinforcement of many of the fiction writer's attitudes and perceptions. Frost was able to formulate and give intellectual authority to such values as individual effort and responsibility that Stegner, out of his frontier past, already felt but had not at the beginning of their friendship fully articulated. But perhaps even more important to Stegner's writing, Frost seems to have imbued his protégé with an ironic stance in regard to human nature and a more tolerant, yet distanced view of human fallibility. He seems to have reinforced Stegner's own lack of sentimentality: as he wrote in a tribute to his mentor, "The real jolt and force of Frost's love of life comes from the fact that it is cold at the root" ("Robert Frost"). And Frost would also seem to have given further validation to Stegner's tendency to find drama and meaningful conflict in ordinary lives.

That glow, that sense of Vermont as a special place that both writers shared, is reflected in a Stegner story, "The Sweetness of the Twisted Apples," that more directly than most other of his fictions illustrates the extent to which Frost influenced his language and perceptions. He wrote the story nearly 10 years after he first met the poet, after he had an opportunity to become familiar with the Vermont countryside and its people firsthand. He and Mary often took off on walks or got in the car and drove around, exploring, more or less aimlessly, in an effort to learn about the area. The story is about such a couple, also summer people, who drive down a track, hardly a road any more, on a voyage of discovery, although their ostensible purpose is to find suitable landscapes for the husband's painting. He is the artist, but it is his wife, Margaret, who is sensitive and open to experience. As they travel further and further away from the paved road, it seems as if they are also traveling back in time. Margaret spots an old stone wall that within a few feet bent off to the right and was swallowed in an impenetrable brush.

Margaret turned and stared back, but the wall did not appear again. It was lost in the woods, still carefully enclosing some obliterated and overgrown meadow, and all the labor that had built it was gone for the greater comfort of woodchucks and foxes. "It doesn't seem as if anything in America could be this old," she said. (*Collected Stories*, 222)

"It doesn't seem as if" is typical Frost syntax, and the passage as a whole, with its perception of nature reclaiming what man has built, may remind us of Frost poems like "The Last Mowing," where the trees, in a shadowy march, threaten to take over a meadow that will no longer be mowed, or "The Wood-Pile," where vines and decay threaten to obliterate a cord of firewood left by someone in the woods—both are traces of man-created order, like the wall spotted by the woman in the story, that will gradually fail and disappear in the inevitable processes of nature: "Something there is that doesn't love a wall," to cite another poem.

The couple in the story go along the road and encounter a mother and daughter—strange country people isolated from the world who may remind us of such Frost characters as the mother and son in "The Witch of Coös," also isolated by place and time, whom he calls "two old believers." The daughter's, Sary's, sad tale of love lost in the passage of time is reminiscent of the recitation of love and youthful hope remembered by the woman in Frost's "The Pauper Witch of Grafton." But Sary's tale is not just sad—she shows considerable day-to-day courage to endure despite her fate. The one beau that she had (she is gnome-like with a pinched face) dropped her to marry someone else and then came to live with his wife just down the road, her only neighbors. Her equanimity in the face of what she calls "her disappointment," her unwillingness to whine or complain—these were traits that both Frost and Stegner admired.

Both Wallace Stegner and Robert Frost shared a deep sense of man's mortality, his fragility in the face of natural or social forces beyond his control, and the necessity to confront the inevitability of decay, neglect, and death—provide, provide. Neither writer would endorse Fra Lippo Lippi's enthusiasm for aging, "The best is yet to be." For them, as for Emily Dickinson, nature can be mysterious and often vaguely threatening to man—dark, like the bottom of a well. In that connection we find that there is often in Stegner's fiction that sense of "haunting" so common to Frost's poetry. Again, the example can be taken from his story

"The Sweetness of the Twisted Apples." While her husband paints, the wife strolls up the road through a deserted village to a burying ground where she stops and sits on a gravestone. She thinks about the gradual abandonment of the area over the years so that at last "there would be a day when you would come to your door and see nothing alive, hear no human sound, in your whole village" (226). Unlike her unseeing husband—ironically, the painter—she is attuned to the vibrations behind appearances:

> She stood up uneasily. A hawk was methodically coursing the meadow beyond the graveyard. It was very still. She felt oppressed by the wide silent sky and afraid of the somehow threatening edge where meadow met woods, where not a leaf stirred but where something watched. (226)

Here is an apprehension familiar to readers of Robert Frost's poems. We see it, among many places, in "The Fear," "Storm Fear," "An Old Man's Winter Night," and "The Hill Wife," poems where something threatening lies just beyond the familiar, where some tenor of the environment strikes apprehension or even terror in the heart of the sensitive observer. Although the threat is ostensibly outside in nature, the subtext is that there is also something inside man himself that can under the right circumstances be brought back to the primitive. In this we are reminded of the Stegner story "The View from the Balcony," where the roars of a lion penetrate the darkness during a party meant to celebrate a student's passing his Ph.D. exam, roars that punctuate the ongoing displays at the party of primitive human emotion.

In both Stegner's and Frost's work joy does come occasionally in man's interaction with nature. Often in Frost moments of joy come when the speaker in the poem has a sudden apprehension of natural beauty, as in "Rose Pogonias," where the speaker and his companions discover "a thousand orchises" among the grass of a meadow. They "raised a simple prayer" that the mowers might spare this spot while the flowers still bloomed.[19] In Stegner's "The Sweetness of the Twisted Apples" joy comes to the wife when she discovers the deformed apples left hanging from the trees in an abandoned orchard. She picks one, tries it, and exclaims with delight at her discovery—they're absolutely delicious. Her husband dismisses her enthusiasm and jokes about the Garden of Eden, but she decides to gather as many apples as she can to fill the whole back of their car and take them home for cider. The metaphor here, so similar to Frost's in "After Apple-Picking," of apples gathered as tokens of experience, suggests once again that the woman is open, able to get beyond surface appearances, and, unlike her husband, can gather experience unto herself and savor it.

One finds also in both writers the joy of work close to nature. We see this in Frost's "Two Tramps in Mud Time," where the speaker is reluctant to give up his task of splitting wood to the two men who come looking for work. Or we see it in "Mowing," in the pleasure of doing a job right, engaged in the actuality of the work, so that the mower concludes: "Anything more than the truth would have seemed too weak / To the earnest love that laid the swale in rows" (*Complete Poems*, 25). Similarly, the boy in Stegner's story "Saw Gang" (1945) finds satisfaction in performing his job well:

> When Donald Swain breathed his lungs full of air, shifted his axe to the other shoulder, and said, "Good workin' weather," the boy looked at him and they grinned. It was what he wanted to say himself. (*Collected Stories*, 70)

"Saw Gang" is also a Vermont story, one that has its roots in Stegner's continuing experience in the area. Going back for a moment to his life story, he had left Wisconsin after only two years for the same reasons that he had left Utah—he had no immediate prospect for promotion and obtaining a tenure-track professorship. Through his acquaintance-ship with Ted Morrison, who was not only the director at Bread Loaf but also head of the writing program at Harvard, Stegner was able to get a job at the Ivy League university, where he began teaching in 1939. Morrison had designed a writing program, containing both freshman composition and advanced courses, wherein his teachers would be published writers. He felt that both the university and the writers would gain from the association. Stegner had by this time, 1939, published not only his award-winning novelette but a number of short stories, and he was on the brink of publishing his first full-length novel (*On a Darkling Plain* [1940]).

After several years at Harvard, he received a small grant from the university and decided he could take the 1942–1943 school year off from teaching in order to try to finish *The Big Rock Candy Mountain*. He decided he could afford to do so if he took up the Grays' offer to stay in their summer home in Vermont over the winter rent-free. He had planned to supply his own firewood and that fall he joined one of the local farmers, George Hill, in a wood-sawing project from which he would take a share. On a number of occasions in previous years, Wallace had helped out with house repairs, barn-raisings, and hay mowing when asked by neighbors, including Hill. Every day for several weeks in the early fall, Wallace went up into the woods on the Hill farm and manned one end of a crosscut saw or swung a double-edged axe from noon until dark (he always spent the mornings, seven days a week, on his manuscript). It was tough work for a man who sat at a desk most of the time nowadays, but it was also satisfying to keep up with Hill and show him that he had as much country in him as Hill had. It was a good fall. He wrote the Grays:

> For two months I've been thinking of nothing but wood, cabbages, carrots, potatoes, apples, and home-canned vegetables. I write my three hours in a dream, eat lunch in a fog, saw wood all afternoon in a sun that's like May, in weather so perfect the air is like wine, it really is, and now I believe the novels. Then I read a book for a couple of hours while Mary darns socks, and we fall into bed exhausted at nine-thirty. It's a marvelous life, only it's like living in a badger hole. I guess I'm Frost's "Drumlin Woodchuck."[20]

That feeling of satisfaction of hard work well done is at the center of the story "Saw Gang" (1945), which he wrote based on his experiences that fall.

The story's center of consciousness is Ernie, "a big boy," in Frost's words about a similar character in his poem "Out, Out . . . ," "doing a man's work, though a child at heart" (*Complete* Poems, 171). Ernie has known the others in the saw gang all his life, but he doesn't yet belong. He has to prove himself (just as Stegner did, but for different reasons) to this close-knit group of country folk, men who have volunteered to help a neighbor and who scorn those from the city who are unskilled in country ways. The men start early, talk little, and work steadily and hard. They chop down the trees with double-bladed axes, roll the logs down to a buzz saw that cuts them into lengths, and then they split the rounds. At one point—the only moment of drama in the story—the saw bucks after hitting a hard knot and throws off the lever holding the log so that it hits one of the men, Will, in the jaw. Will makes light of it, and the men have lunch and go back to work.

The story ends with the boy looking at what they had accomplished and knowing "that they had done a day's work that amounted to something" (74), that the farmer they were helping had enough wood there to last him for two years. As they gather up their things and head down the hill, Ernie's

> back ached as if a log had dropped across it, and a hard sore spot had developed under his left shoulder blade, but he followed them out of the woods feeling good, feeling tired and full of October smell and the smell of fresh-sawed wood and hot oil. (*Collected Stories*, 74)

On the way down, one of the men looks at the "chewed and whittled spruce butts" left by a "city boy" that the farmer had hired the previous summer to do some clearing along the road. Rather than cut cleanly, they had been mangled with a dull axe and then finally just broken off. The man shakes his head in wonder at the sight and laughs. The implication is that by comparison to this other boy, Ernie now belongs to those who know how to do such a job right.

"Belonging" is a common theme in Stegner's work—we see it in such other stories as "In the Twilight," "The Chink," and "Balance His, Swing Yours"—a theme that once again comes out of the emotions of his own life, as a boy and teenager who was cut off from others by his father's occupation. "Saw Gang" has virtually no plot, but it does have "wholeness, harmony and radiance," in the words of Stephen Dedalus, quoting Aquinas in *A Portrait of the Artist as a Young Man*, a radiance that convinces us, as in many Stegner stories, that although not much seems to have happened, a whole lot has.

Another story, "The Traveler," also comes out of Stegner's experiences in the Greensboro area. He and Mary drove up from Cambridge to Vermont and were staying at the Grays' on a skiing trip during the winter of 1941–1942. "It was," he recalled years later, "about 20 below, everyone had the flu, the car wouldn't start, and I had to walk about two miles to town . . . to get some help." As he walked through "a magical kind of moonlight," he was reminded of his own childhood in Saskatchewan—suddenly he was transported back in time. He felt he had done this before and he had been "here" before (Kazak, 29). In the story, as the central characters walks in the starlight,

> something long buried and forgotten tugged in him and a shiver not entirely from cold prickled his whole body with gooseflesh. There had been times in his childhood when he had walked home alone and had been temporarily lost in nights like this. . . . He felt spooked. (*Collected Stories*, 5)

The story concerns a pharmaceutical salesman whose car breaks down at night out in the country, in the snow. At first he waits for a passing car, but none comes and he decides to walk and look for a farmhouse. But having set out to find help for himself, he is the one who must give help when he finally reaches a farm and finds a boy, anxious and desperate, whose grandfather has fallen ill. How could the author's experience of recognizing a feeling from childhood be translated into a story about a medicine supply salesman whose car breaks down on a lonely country road? The question was asked at a bookstore reading set up to publicize the publication of his *Collected Stories*, and the author replied, "Don't trust the details—trust the feeling" (Kazak, 29).

In "The Traveler" as the salesman's situation becomes increasingly more desperate, he begins not only to experience some fear, but also resentment. He thinks of where he should be—comfortably bathed, fed, and in his warm hotel room. He thinks,

> For all of this to be torn away suddenly, for him to be stumbling up a deserted road in danger of freezing to death, just because some simple mechanical part that had functioned for thirty thousand miles refused to function any longer, this was outrage, and he hated it. (*Collected Stories*, 6)

The tone and emotion here is reminiscent of the correspondent in Stephen Crane's "The Open Boat," who protests,

> If I am going to be drowned—if I am going to be drowned—if I am going to be drowned, why, in the name of the seven mad gods who rule the sea, was I allowed to come thus far and contemplate sand and trees.[21]

The salesman, too, through the failure of a mechanical device (a ship for the correspondent), is cast to the whims of a merciless, indifferent nature. Both stories depend on the archetype of the journey, a journey through the elements, the sea and snow, which threaten death at any moment. And in the Crane and Stegner stories the extremity of the protagonists' situations are underlined by a comparison with life as it might have been, or should have been, in the comfort of shore, or, in the case of the salesman, the comfort of his hotel room.

Rescue, more than physically, comes in both stories as a result of the discovery by the protagonists of their bonds of brotherhood with other men. And in both stories the recognition of that bond comes in a changing of perspective. For the correspondent in "The Open Boat" that change comes when, after finding himself in a lifeboat with three other men, surrounded by the threatening sea, he realizes how dependent on each other they have become. For the traveler the change comes when he sees himself in the boy and determines that he must help him.

The beginnings of the change for the salesman come in a scene where his fear is changed to an apprehension of radiance with the appearance of the moon. This is a moment of enlightenment, of "warmth"—he is about to be taken out of his need to be rescued into the role of rescuer. In this moment the entire perspective is altered (both stories are in part about perception—how we see things and why). As the salesman approaches a farmhouse he encounters a boy stumbling out of a barn, where he had been hitching a horse to a sleigh in order to get help for his grandfather. In this meeting with the boy, the salesman seems to meet himself at the same age. The kitchen is familiar in all its smells: "The ways a man fitted in with himself and with other human beings were curious and complex" (*Collected Stories*, 10). As he takes the sleigh to get help at the Hill farm, 2 miles down the road, the salesman

> looked back once, to fix forever the picture of himself standing silently watching himself go. . . . For from the most chronic and incurable of ills, identity, he had looked outward and for one unmistakable instant recognized himself. (11)

"The Traveler," as well as "Saw Gang" and "The Sweetness of the Twisted Apples," might be thought of as "landscapes with figures." The same thing is true of such early Stegner stories as "Bugle Song" and "Two Rivers." What they all have in common is a story that is very visual, where the setting is important and the mood presented by the setting is central to the essential effect. In fact, the setting, or at least the characters' interaction with the setting, *is* the story. At the same time there is very little plot in these stories, often so little that they are nearly without event. Not much happens. One could almost say that such stories are more like paintings than works of fiction as normally defined.

This painterly quality can also be found in another of Stegner's stories set in Vermont, "The Berry Patch," and in fact the landscape and emotion of the story might remind us of an actual painting—Andrew Wyeth's "The Berry Picker." The location in the story is the top of a hill overlooking Caspian Lake and the village of Greensboro, Vermont, a frequent picnic spot in real life for the Stegners and their friends. The characters are Alma and Perley Hill ("Hill" is a name frequently used by Stegner in his Vermont stories and is taken from a farm family in the area with several branches with several farms). Perley is a farmer who, during World War II, has been away in the army and is home temporarily on furlough. Alma, his wife, has been left alone to try to make the farm go while her husband has been away.

The situation is emotionally charged. We know, as Alma knows, that Perley will be going back to being a soldier, with all that implies: he may be maimed and not be able to do the physical work of the farm, or he may not even come back from the war. After he leaves, she will have to go back to struggling to maintain the farm herself. We know that after the war, even if Perley returns intact, their lives will not be easy (we learn this indirectly from the references to all the neighboring farms that have failed and neighbors who have left the area). In the face of this background of struggle and worry, this brief outing in the woods, this brief respite from a world at war, becomes even more treasured. Time becomes a major theme because this moment, now, becomes timeless, etched in their bones, whereas the implications of the past (their relationship), the immediate past (their separation by war and the awkwardness of their reunion), and the future (the difficulties of keeping the farm going in an area of failing farms and hardship) are implicit throughout the present of the story.

"The Berry Patch" is touching without being sentimental, the emotion carefully controlled by the characterizations of two country people who don't talk directly about their emotions and who are restrained in the expression of their affection for each other. That contrast between what we know they must feel and their reluctance to express those feelings openly, a type of verbal irony, is likely to increase the emotional response on the part of the reader. Intensifying the emotion also is the emphasis in the story on the value of simple things. We witness this couple reunited after a forced separation and being together within the simple experience of gathering berries in the warmth of the sun and beauty of the countryside. There is nothing complicated or sophisticated here, only exposure to the simple things of life—gentleness, caring, companionship, mutual concern, and an intimate connection with nature (all muted, all expressed implicitly), and an expedition to gather berries as an excuse for an outing. How valuable, how precious, and, alas, how temporary such things may seem to be one day on a hillside in the sun and wind.

And yet these simple things are also lasting, not only etched into the psyches of the characters, but recorded as painting. The story is not so much a linear narrative, as a filling out of the picture by completing the canvas and giving those dimensions to the figures in the landscape through the skill of the author that transmit the painting's spiritual-emotional power. The characters' sense of place, *where* they are, is ultimately important: they are near their farm and in an area where they have been all their lives and belong. Not only their livelihood but their very identities depend on where they are.

A pronouncement by Stegner's former student Wendell Berry fits this story as one considers the story a demonstration of a sense of place. He has said, and Stegner has often quoted him, "If you don't know where you are, you don't know who you are."[22] Like Perley and Alma, Berry is a farmer, a man who gave up a promising career as a creative writing teacher at an elite university to go back to the land farmed by several generations of his family. If there is any plot to "The Berry Patch" at all, it lies in the process of rediscovery by this couple of each other after their separation by the war. Perley has been out of touch and is trying to get in touch with his wife again, a somewhat tentative and awkward process. He is tender, but yet questioning; he is worried about her situation—how is she getting along on her own?—but doesn't want to make her think he doubts her abilities. For both husband and wife, it is a process of rediscovery made possible by identities reconfirmed by place.

That place is described in loving detail throughout the story by someone very familiar with it, someone who has also picked berries on Barr Hill:

> When she got to his side he was standing among knee-high bushes, and all down the falling meadow, which opened on the west into a clear view of the valley, the village, the lake, the hills beyond hills and the final peaks, the dwarf bushes were so laden that the berries gleamed through the covering leaves like clusters of tiny flowers. (*Collected Stories*, 36)

And the landscape itself becomes a metaphor, not only for Alma and Perley's rediscovery of the joy of their relationship but for the survival of their farm, their will to make a go of it, and their love in the face of war and economic difficulty: "More you plow it up, the more berries there is next year. Burn it over, it's up again before anything else" (38). When Alma shows her husband her bucket full of berries and says, "I got quite a mess.... How about you?" He replies, " 'All I want.' ... He was watching the sun dapple the brown skin of her throat as the wind bent the thin tops of the maples. 'I wouldn't want any more,' he said" (39).

Back to the West and Travel Stories

Much to Wallace's delight he was promoted—for the first time in his career—and received tenure at Harvard in 1943. He could have stayed on, but neither he nor his wife much liked the prospect of remaining in the East permanently, and he began to look around in the West for another teaching position. This change of direction after such good fortune may sound strange, but it underlines his sense of place: he was a dyed-in-the-wool westerner by habit of thought and affection. As much as the Stegners enjoyed the cultural advantages and their friends in Cambridge, they simply did not feel at home there. Then in 1944 Wallace got an offer from *Look* magazine, at a much higher salary than he was earning at Harvard, to write a series of articles about prejudice in the United States which would, after magazine publication, be published as a book.

He took a leave of absence from Harvard and began the research for his articles. The plan was to travel around the United States and interview members of various racial and religious groups that had suffered from discrimination. One advantage to the job was that he was able to get out and around the country for the first time in years. His assignment provided gasoline ration stamps when travel was severely limited during the war effort. Working his way first from north to south and then east to west, he visited the South and wrote about Jim Crow, and then about the northern migration of blacks. He went to cities in the East and wrote about Jews in America and their role as scapegoats. He went to Indian reservations in Oklahoma and the Southwest, and to a Trappist Monastery in the Midwest.

As his research took him more and more westward, he and Mary relocated to Santa Barbara, where, between trips, he would do much of the writing itself. From Santa Barbara he traveled to the Japanese relocation camps in Nevada, to the Sacramento Valley to interview Filipinos, and to the San Joaquin Valley where he stayed with Mexican crop-workers. He spent some time in Los Angeles, where *Look* had offices, coordinating his work with that of the photographers who would illustrate the articles.

Also in Los Angeles he met a social worker, whose caseload included young blacks and Mexican Americans, and he followed her on her rounds, off and on, for several weeks. Based on his experiences with her, he wrote the essay "Lost Generation: The Pachucos of Los Angeles," and two short stories. The stories are two of only a very few Stegner wrote that have urban settings. The first of these, "Pop Goes the Alley Cat," is about a white photographer who accompanies a social worker on her rounds in the Mexican barrio of Los Angeles. In the experiences and reactions of the photographer, Charlie Prescott, we see the ambivalence of the white liberal as his sympathy is stretched to the breaking point. As Charlie and Carol, the social worker, go out to photograph conditions in the barrio, they run into Johnny Bane, an angry young black who is one of her charges and who is always in trouble and can't hold a job. He is helplessly caught up in a cycle of violence that Carol, by giving him trust and encouragement, is trying to break.

After taking pictures of one family, Charlie gives in to Johnny's suggestion that they might get some good shots at the home of his Mexican girlfriend. There, a ruckus breaks out when in response to the girl's teasing, Johnny calls her a name. To cool the situation off, Carol sends Johnny in her car to the store to get some cigarettes. After another photo session in a hovel where the sickness is so bad and unattended that Charlie takes it upon himself to go to a phone both to call a doctor, Charlie comes back and realizes that Johnny has taken one of his cameras with him and still has not returned from his errand.

He and Carol sit and wait for Johnny to come back, an unlikely possibility now. Charlie is

> abruptly furious with her. Social betterment, sure, opportunities, yes, a helping hand, naturally. But to lie down and let a goon like that walk all over you, abuse your confidence, lie and cheat and steal and take advantage of every unselfish gesture! (*Collected Stories,* 262)

Carol admits that Johnny is everything that Charlie says he is, but Johnny has told her "things," namely, that he pops the necks of stray cats when they won't let themselves be petted. She says, "You can't say, 'I gave him every chance,' unless you really did" (244). The narrator realizes that from her point of view, "You could not put limits on love— if love was what you chose to live by" (265).

The focus of the story, of course, is not Johnny so much as it is Charlie's white liberal attitudes. As it is in so many of Stegner's stories and novels, the problem is one of "getting one's head straight," which usually involves a re-examination of one's thinking processes and feelings. Stegner has picked out precisely a prime difficulty of race relations, relations between middle-class whites and poor blacks, a difficulty that many whites are incapable of seeing. Middle-class whites, with the best of intentions, want dispossessed blacks to participate and achieve in society on *white terms*: everything, including compassion and understanding, is strictly limited, defined by white expectations. They want to dole out help and compassion in little neat packages with instructions sheets, and if the instructions are not followed exactly, no more packages are given. Furthermore, the story demonstrates that prejudice and distrust is not just a white failing, but a human failing shared by blacks and Hispanics as well. They too put all kinds of limits, out of their own cultural backgrounds, on their willingness to be tolerant of others.

A second story, "He Who Spits at the Sky," has two of the same characters as the first: Charlie Prescott, the professional photographer, and Carol, the social worker. However, the two take on roles more as observers than actors in this story. They have been invited to a party at Guy and Debbie Mazur's house in Hollywood to celebrate the release from San Quentin of the "Red Car Kids," three Mexican-American young men who have been presumably railroaded to jail for a murder they did not commit. But shadowing their release is the awareness that as gang members they have been also presumably guilty of many other crimes. Guy Mazur, the host, and a committee of "socially concerned" liberals-radicals are there to plan a campaign to use to the young men to forward their own political agenda.

At the party Debbie, Guy's trophy wife, is put down repeatedly by her husband, and she rebels by kissing and dancing with all the Chicano boys. Her husband thinks that she is not too bright, but she is smart enough to understand that he is just using the boys for his own purposes: "Mazur thinks he made you all out of tin and wound you up. . . . He thinks he made me out of tin and wound me up, too" (500). Carol, the social worker, sees all this and is worried that Debbie's behavior will somehow get the boys in trouble and tries to sidetrack the confrontations she thinks will come.

Guy is so involved with his "do-gooders," as Debbie puts it, that he misses all the byplay, particularly the reactions of the boys' girlfriends. One of them, Angelina, has become visibly angry in response to Debbie's flirtations with Pepe. In a darkened room, Pepe tries to kiss

Angelina, who resists, and he ends up socking her in the face, splitting her lips from chin to nose. Charlie witnesses everything, but Pepe denies hitting her. Guy tries to figure out how to handle the situation without upsetting his plans. Charlie accuses Pepe in front of the group, but Dago, who has also witnessed the act from the doorway, refuses to back Charlie, making the silent gesture to him of spitting at the sky. "It wouldn't do any good" or "what's the use" seems to be Dago's message, not, only in regard to this specific situation, but one of helplessness in regard to his life in general, whether he is caught up in the activities of the gang or simply a pawn in Guy Mazur's political gamesmanship. The sadness of the story rests with the realization of Dago's entrapment. Of the three boys he is the one who is most promising as someone who could make something of himself. He is good-looking and intelligent, but also a young man with a conscience, but a conscience he obviously does not feel free to exercise in a no-win situation.

These two stories are not only different from Stegner's other stories in their urban settings but also in their subject matter as developed within those settings—social problems and social responsibility, political maneuvering, racial minorities, and the social pressure to conform. Some of these subjects, however, we have seen evolve into themes in other contexts. The pressure to conform, for example, is at the heart of the boy's unhappiness with his outlaw family in "The Volunteer" or, as translated into the awareness of not belonging, the realization of Mr. Hart in "Balance His, Swing Yours." And while we don't see it in many of the stories, the theme of manipulation by the cold calculation of the political radical is common to many of Stegner's novels, including *Fire and Ice*, *Joe Hill*, *All the Little Live Things*, and *The Spectator Bird*. Stegner was a middle-of-the-road liberal and hated fanaticism and extremism of any variety as not only destructive of individuals, but of a democratic society. A person using another person for his own ends was anathema to him.

Stegner himself came out of an impoverished background, socially and financially, but in an entirely different setting, and it is clear that his experiences researching for the *Look* articles opened up new vistas of concern for him. One of his first research projects for his new job was to uncover as much as he could about violence against Jews in South Boston. Gangs of Irish youths were regularly setting upon and beating up Jewish boys, and no one in authority seemed willing to do anything about it. The resulting article, "Who Persecutes Boston?", which took to task both the Catholic Church and police for their inaction, turned out to be too hot for *Look* to handle, and the article eventually appeared in the *Atlantic*. As a result, the *Look* editors decided to change the plan. He was to go ahead and write his articles and although *Look* would not publish them, he would be free to publish them wherever he could. However, the magazine would retain the right at the end of his research and writing to gather the articles together and publish them as a book, which it considered less threatening to its circulation. This it did in *One Nation* (1945), but only after a considerable editorial softening of Stegner's pointed analysis.

After several months finishing up work on the book at *Look* headquarters in New York, Wallace and Mary returned to Santa Barbara, where Wallace tried to relax and recover from a heart infection and a general sense of exhaustion. He had already obtained a new teaching job at Stanford University where in the fall of 1945 he would begin developing a new creative writing program as well as teaching American literature. Out of habit, he went out every morning to sit at his desk in a room that he had adopted as his study in their little house. He had no specific projects in mind, and idly, he spent a lot of time looking out his window. After a couple of days an idea for a story came to him, an idea that evolved into "The Women on the Wall," a story that would have a profound influence on the further direction of his fiction.

The story features Mr. Palmer, a figure vaguely reminiscent of Stegner himself, who is in late middle age, retired, and writing his memoirs in a house near the Pacific Ocean. He is courtly in manner and, even in 1945, seems out of his time in a present more violent, full of conflict, less genteel, and less polite than he seems to expect. Just as the author was doing when he got the idea for the story, Palmer spends much of his time looking out his window. (This is also a preoccupation of his successor, Joe Allston, in the second of these postwar germinal stories, "Field Guide to the Western Birds.")

Although the story is not told in the first person, but in the third-person, limited-omniscient point of view that had been a Stegner favorite, the center of consciousness, Mr. Palmer, is nevertheless the earliest appearance of what might be called the elderly writer-observer figure who is the most common protagonist of Stegner's late fiction. Palmer is experienced, sensitive to his environment, an observer of people, a bit skeptical and self-doubting, and despite a somewhat hardened shell, vulnerable to emotion—all qualities that would be carried over, although in somewhat different proportions, to Joe Allston in "Field Guide," *All the Little Live Things*, and *Spectator Bird*; Lyman Ward in *Angle of Repose*; and Larry Morgan in *Crossing to Safety*. And while these later characters have a romantic streak, Palmer's romanticism is so extreme it carries him into fundamental errors about the people he observes. This is a harsh, almost shocking story about perception and the discovery of what is real.

Palmer looks out his study window at the women who line up every day along a wall across the point overlooking the ocean. These are Army and Navy wives who, during the latter stages of World War II, are waiting at their mailboxes for word of their husbands, and out of bookishness, Palmer is reminded of Homer's Penelope "on the rocky isle of Ithaca above the wine-dark sea," and he finds himself getting "a little sentimental about these women" (42). Of course, the point of the story depends on the unreliability of his perceptual framework—the women, on closer acquaintance, turn out to be very unromantic figures indeed. One of his Penelopes turns out to be a dope addict who is willing to neglect her young daughter in favor of a fix; another, insecure and hysterical, smothers her child with overprotectiveness; another, unmarried, has become pregnant and worries that her lover may not come back and "make a decent woman" of her. They are backbiting, self-involved, and in conflict with one another—not at all the placid, patient, heroic figures Palmer has imagined them to be and has admired.

To a lesser extent the narrators of "Field Guide to the Western Birds" and the later novels—Joe Allston, Lyman Ward, and Larry Morgan—are also unreliable in their perceptions, and they, too, want to place the people around them as players in their personally scripted dramas, dramas that reflect their own preconceptions, prejudices, and desires. This tendency contributes to a theme related to the discovery of reality behind appearances—identity, our own (that is, the self-discovery of the narrator or center of consciousness) and others (that is, the characters observed by the narrator). As in "The Women on the Wall," each of the later novels carried by these first-person narrators has as its central concern an effort to understand and make a judgment about a major character in that novel, a pattern prefigured not only in "The Women on the Wall" (where Palmer is led to make judgments about several characters), but in "Field Guide to the Western Birds" as well. In making their judgments—Palmer and the novel protagonists—they identify and characterize themselves to the reader, who in turn judges them.

However, each of the narrators in the late novels finds himself in a position where he is not only unsure of precisely what judgment to make, but unsure about his own ability or qualifications to make that judgment. Mr. Palmer, by contrast, seems so certain of his own vision that both he and the reader are startled by his mistake, and the thought that sticks with us from the story is the complete failure of the center of consciousness to see things as they really are. Ultimately, Palmer's fussiness and egocentricity alienate us and his errors are so gross that we cannot trust or believe in him.

In an essay called "A Problem in Fiction," the author tells how he wrote the story, a rare look into his process of composition. "The Women on the Wall" was not one of those that sometimes mysteriously seems to write itself, but one that had to be hewn out step by step by main force. The scene viewed by Mr. Palmer was a scene that Stegner saw out of his own study window while wondering what project he would start on next:

> Before two mornings had passed, what I really did in my study was watch that most beautiful, lulled, enchanted place above the blue and violet sea, with the frieze of bright, still women along the wall.
>
> I have no idea at what point I began to think of them as a story. It was simply apparent after awhile that I felt them with the clarity and force of a symbol, and that I wanted to write them. But you did not write a picture. You do not even write a "situation."[23]

He was on his way to writing a story—he had a place, a group of people, a situation, even a classical parallel (Penelope waiting for Ulysses)—but he had no idea what the story was going to be about.

He tried to force action on the women, but that didn't work; he tried bringing in some invented suitors, following *Ulysses*, but they were out of place; and then he tried a kind of Grand Hotel scheme, following each woman and her husband to a conclusion, but that got to be too long and complicated—an idea, perhaps, for a novel, but he had no intention of writing a novel about this scene. Then it became clear to him "that these women fascinated me precisely because they did nothing but wait" and that he should concentrate on the effects of waiting on them and that there should not be a single line of action, but a series of uncoverings:

> The problem, I finally began to see, was not to make action out of this picture, but by moving the picture slightly to reveal what was hidden behind it. This story would develop, certainly, not as a complication resolved but as what Henry James called a "situation revealed."

And if revealed, it must be revealed to someone. I had already tried, with a dismal sense of failure, to get at these women from the inside. In the end I adopted the point of view that was at once easiest and most natural—my own, the viewpoint of the external observer. ("Problem," 372)

This persona, Mr. Palmer, tries to make acquaintance with the women and is rebuffed. The author needed to devise something to bring Mr. Palmer close to them again, and fate provided Stegner with a real-life incident in the form of a cocker spaniel that appeared one day tied to a tree, barking and howling, and then at sunset mysteriously disappearing. Stegner brought the dog into the story and used it not only as a means to bring Palmer into the company of the women but to lead to a characterization of one of the women, Mrs. Kendall, and to symbolically represent "the way everybody in the story, adult, child, or dog, was tied down helplessly and no relief for it" ("Problem," 374). Through another woman, Mrs. Corson, who gets high on marijuana and becomes talkative, the conditions of the other women are exposed to Palmer, and the "idyllic and wistful picture [he] started with has been violently shoved aside and the turmoil of suffering and frustrated humanity it has covered is revealed" (374).

What is most interesting in this description is the interplay of experience and imagination in the creative process, how the original scene—the smell of pine and eucalyptus and wood smoke and kelp; the sound of the surf on the beach; and the sight of the women waiting quietly and patiently for the mail—stimulated the writer. First he was reminded of literary parallels, not only of Penelope on the rocky isle of Ithaca above the wine-dark sea, but of Keats's "Ode on a Grecian Urn." In both cases a situation very dramatic was encapsulated, waiting to be revealed by the poets' imagination. Second, he was led to realize that he, too, must stay with the picture and by moving it slightly and letting his imagination work, "reveal what was hidden behind it."

Many details came to him out of ongoing experience—the barking dog—or recent experience—Mrs. Corson smokes marijuana because, having just interviewed Mexican youths in Los Angeles, Stegner "had marijuana on [his] mind." In regard to such details, he notes that

so much of what attaches itself or insinuates itself when one is making a story is purest accident; the story growing in the mind becomes a kind of flypaper that catches everything light, everything loose. (373)

69

As readers or critics, we are all too likely to think of the essence of a story and its details as the result of a much more conscious and deliberate process than is actually the case. We see connections, an underlying pattern, and we just assume that in writing a particular text the author does the same—consciously seeking to apply "his theme" to a particular occasion.

It never seems to have occurred to Stegner in looking back on the composition of this story, that his theme here, the revelation of stark reality behind romantic appearances, was a common one in his work. He didn't start with that theme as a goal, but came to it after a struggle, unconsciously. What seems to be fundamental to his process was an attitude—a skepticism, a suspicion of smooth exteriors, and a conviction that there is always more to a situation than appears on the surface, and indeed he says at one point in his essay, "I thought that their [the women's] quiet could not possibly be more than skin-deep, that beneath their muted surface must be a seethe and dart of emotion like a school of small fish just under the unbroken surface of water" (372). It was a similar conviction that of course tied together such disparate authors of the Realistic Period as Henry James and Mark Twain, Edith Wharton and Theodore Dreiser, and it was the Realistic Period that was Stegner's specialty as a teacher of American literature. In respect to the theme of discovering what lies beneath the surface, one can see "The Women on the Wall" as a clear preface to *Angle of Repose* and *The Spectator Bird*. Both of his prize-winning novels are novels of discovery.

As noted earlier, Stegner's short stories were largely produced during two bursts of activity, from 1938 to 1943 and from 1947 to 1958. "The Women on the Wall" (1946), published between the two periods, was among several exceptions to these groupings, as was another story, "The Volcano" (1944). It came out of a vacation trip that Wallace and Mary made to Mexico just after his leaving Harvard and before taking on the *Look* assignment. "The Volcano" can be considered the first of a subgrouping that was produced during the later period—stories that came out of his travels. After taking on the job at Stanford, Stegner went on several extended trips abroad, and situations and characters that he encountered on these trips inspired a number of other stories that may seem at odds with his later reputation as "the dean of western writers."

Most of these travel stories, and certainly "The Volcano," have as one of their central themes the conflict of American with foreign cultures. The American protagonist finds himself learning something about other people, but also about himself, and in the confrontation of one culture with another, he is usually humbled by his encounter. In one way or another he discovers his ignorance, an ignorance that suggests that he is, as an American, so involved in the modern and technological, that he has been removed from the land and from the sympathetic vibrations that the natives of a region have with nature. He is, in effect, taken back to basics and forced by his experiences to reevaluate his outlook and values. This theme, to some extent, reflects the progress of Stegner's own life, from a childhood close to the land where his family was forced to live on a subsistence level, to a sophisticated life of comfort and convenience as an adult. In these stories he not only seems to be regressing in cultural time but seems to be recovering his own more challenging and earth-connected past and its values. As we have seen in the case of "The Traveler" this recovery is essentially nostalgic; in these travel stories, however, the confrontation with a more basic way of life can be distressing, even painful.

The narrator of "The Volcano" is significantly called only "the American." As a tourist he has gone to Paricutin in Mexico, presumably out of curiosity to see the effects of the eruption and the volcano's continuing activity. (In life, the volcano of Paricutin came out of dormancy and erupted in 1943, just a few months before the author had visited the area.) With his Mexican driver and guide, the American approaches within two miles of the volcano and sees it venting "monstrous puffs of black smoke [which] mushroomed upward" (*Collected Stories*, 109). There is nothing nostalgic about this setting; it is like a scene out of hell, "a landscape without shadows, submerged in gray twilight" (112). The village of Paricutin on the other side of the mountain had been completely buried under lava:

> That was death both definite and sudden. But [here in the village of San Juan] this slow death that fell like light rain, the gradual smothering that drooped the pines and covered the holes of the little animals and mounded the roofs and choked the streets, this dying village through which ghosts went in silence, was something else. (111)

As so often is the case in Stegner's work, the landscape becomes invested with emotion. The American tells his driver, "I have conceived a great hatred for this thing. . . . It is a thing I have always known and always hated" (112). It is something, he realizes, that the Mexicans have also always known, or else there would not be the figure of the robed skeleton in so many of their paintings. "They were patient under it, they accepted it" (112), but at the same time he notices two little Indian girls, each with a small baby hung over her back, wading through the knee-deep powder and wonders at how alive their eyes, above the muffling *rebozos*, are—how very alive. There would seem to be a lesson here in adaptation, in the survival of the human spirit under the worst of circumstances by these unsophisticated people. The American has come to the volcano to see something unusual, something wondrous, but the wonder, the touching vision that sticks with him, is the eyes of the little girls, eyes that in their vitality seem to promise hope for the race in a nearly hopeless situation.

The innate wisdom of a more primitive people in response to nature and an acceptance of the ever present threat of death is the subject of another story set on the other side of the world. "The City of the Living" is a powerful account of a father's worry and dread during a night of vigil over a critically ill young son in a foreign country. It is based on an incident that happened in Luxor, Egypt, while the Stegners were on a seven-month trip around the world for the Rockefeller Foundation, that began in September 1950. The purpose of the trip was to establish a postwar connection between writers, particularly American and Asian writers. On their way to the Far East, the Stegner's spent time in Europe and Egypt viewing the wreckage of the war. While they were in Luxor, the Stegners' young son, Page, was stricken with typhoid. The night that the fever came to a climax and broke is the basis for the story. Wallace wrote to his friends, Phil and Peg Gray, from Egypt to report the actual events:

> All through Europe, when we're fooling around, we stay healthy. The minute it comes time to work, Page comes down with typhoid, and here we stick. Fortunately, thanks to Chloromycetin, typhoid is no longer its old self. . . . All last night, while I was sitting up ladling pills into poor Page, the muezzin kept howling from his minaret and every dog and jackal in upper Egypt howled back, and about dawn a baboon or some goddam thing climbed on the balcony and yelled bloody murder. But what a fine river is the Nile and what a picturesque character is the fellaheen.[24]

Reported so matter-of-factly, these were the events out of which the story, written three years later, would grow. Always the reticent and uncomplaining Westerner, Stegner never in his letters, or in conversation for that matter, reveals the true depth of his emotions. These he saves for his stories, and even there they are often stowed in inconspic-uous suitcases that await unpacking by the reader.

Although "The City of the Living" is one of Stegner's most personal stories, the central character, Robert Chapman, has little in common with the author (perhaps based on Robert Frost's advice to Stegner that if a story happened to you, tell it as if it happened to someone else; if the story happened to someone else, tell it as if it happened to you). One change is particularly significant: Chapman is divorced and there-fore must face this crisis alone. The illness of his son, the outside crisis, is only the beginning, the occasion that forces a crisis internally wherein Chapman must acknowledge his past sins and his present aloneness and helplessness. This is a frequent process in Stegner's fiction—self-examination, which leads to self-acknowledgment, which in turn leads to a revelation promising possible change. Often in his fiction, as here, it is not what the central character does that counts but the experience that he undergoes and the actions by others that he observes that become the catalyst for enlightenment.

In this short story we undergo with Chapman a long night of the soul, a vigil during which he must confront the choices he has made and the self he has created. While there are only few overt references to religion there are overtones that suggest this is a religious experience—the night of prayer and fasting that a novitiate must endure before the priesthood or a squire must pass through before being knighted. One such overtone is the sense that although the father puts his faith in antibiotics (if he had to pray to something, that is what, he decides, he would have to pray to), he is haunted by a primitive fear of the unknown and comes to a realization that the struggle between life and death takes place in a zone beyond his control, beyond even his understand-ing, something that as a person who has always striven to control his cir-cumstances makes him profoundly uneasy.

The boy's life and death are balanced on a knife blade, leading to new definitions for the father of both life and living, death and dying. The story is framed in such fundamental contrasts throughout—light and dark, American and foreign, familiar and strange, safe and risky, modern and ancient, clean and dirty—until both the external (the illness of the boy) and internal (the fear and dread of the father) conflicts are re-solved, and with the dawn, the "city of the dead" turns into the "city of the living."

Chapman is a wealthy, self-centered, worldly San Francisco attorney, a member of exclusive clubs, a play-it-safe conservative who takes out plenty of insurance—he not only has insurance, he *likes* insurance—and who, along the same lines, has packed a special bag for medical emergencies overseas. He is a man who doesn't want to take the smallest emotional risks—he was even glad when his wife left him. He may remind us of a Stegner character, Mr. Burns, in another story which came out of the Rockefeller trip, "Something Spurious from the Mindanao Deep." Burns, too, considers anything foreign as possibly dangerous. He will not, for instance, eat the Filipino food and his unwillingness to take risks seems to rob him of life. But, unlike Chapman, Burns does not show the promise of change but ends where he began, as we see in the final metaphor with its potent imagery:

> When the gimlet was on the table before him and its penetrating lime odor was rising to his nostrils as clean as the sniff of Benzedrine from an inhaler, he fished from his shirt pocket the envelope he carried there, and out of its assortment of pills and capsules selected an iron pill, a multi-vitamin capsule, and a concentrated capsule of vitamin C. (*Collected Stories*, 376)

It is clear that in the author's mind this is not living, and it may be that since both these stories deal with the risks, physical and emotional, that these travelers in a foreign country are loath to take, a conflict in Stegner's mind over his own touristlike timidity would seem to have bothered him during his year abroad. More important, however, was his ability to take this conflict, so common to Americans overseas, and make of it a complex metaphor for the risks one must take and the commitment one must make in order that love and living become possible.

In "The City of the Living" the father is seen in the lit bathroom of a hotel with his son lying sick in the bedroom adjoining. The opening time is the oncoming of darkness, and the night signals a time of crisis in his son's fever. All around him seems threatening—the dark, the foreign city, and the noises that suggest that something is looking into the room from the trees outside. He looks with horror at the way the disease has wasted his son in little more than a day, and "he drew into his lungs the inhuman, poisonous stench of the sickness. That was the moment when it first occurred to him that the boy could die" (515). He tries to keep busy and occupy his mind by writing bills and postcards, but he realizes there is no one to whom he can write a letter, certainly not about his real feelings at this moment. "I am just beginning to realize that here or anywhere else I am almost completely alone. I have spent my life avoiding entanglements" (515).

Early in the morning he dozes off and then awakes with a start at 5:30, feeling guilty. His arm aches from a booster shot, and as he takes a drink of water from the carafe,

> the chlorine bite of the halazone tablets gagged him. The effort, the steady, unrelieved, incessant effort that it took in this place to stay alive! He looked at his haggard, smudged face in the mirror and he hated Egypt with a kind of ecstasy. (521)

But when he checks on his son, he finds the crisis is over. It is almost dawn. He is greatly relieved—exultant. Suddenly his perceptions change. Everything looks better. He looks out across the river at the City of the Dead, which the night before seemed so threatening, and sees that it "was innocent and clean now, and the river that when they first came had seemed to him a dirty, mud-banked sewer looked different too" (523).

It is at this point, near the end of the story, that Chapman has a vision that brings to him a realization, joining life and death. Safe now, and relieved of anxiety, he looks down out his window as "all the Nile's creatures, as inexhaustible as the creatures of the sea, began to creep and crawl and fly," watching them from "his little cell of sanitary plumbing, and on his hands as he held the binoculars to his eyes he smelled the persistent odor of antiseptic" (523). He looks out, receptive for the first time to that which is outside his antiseptic circle—a metaphor that extends from the physical to the emotional to the spiritual. He looks down and sees one of the ragged boys who takes care of the garden paths and sees him wash and pray:

> Yet the praying boy was not pathetic or repulsive or ridiculous. His every move was assured, completely natural. His touching of the earth with his forehead made Chapman want somehow to lay a hand on his bent back.
>
> They have more death than we do, Chapman thought. Whatever he is praying to has more death in it than anything we know.
>
> Maybe it had more life too. (524–25)

This boy, of course, is also his boy, as well as all mankind—as we face the darkness of our limitations and the forces of nature, forces that a ring of antiseptic can hardly begin to forestall. We know that Chapman will not change his entire lifestyle, revise all his beliefs, such as they are, or values, but we do believe that at the end of his ordeal he becomes a little more connected to other men and to the earth, that in some way his is better for his experience. The gradual movement in this story toward enlightenment and self-knowledge may well have been a technique that Stegner learned from the story writer he admired most: "Chekhov had a way of turning up the rheostat, little by little . . . Joyce called it an epiphany. Katherine Mansfield called it a nuance" (Shenker). Although "The City of the Living" was sent out by Stegner's agents six times before it found a home in *Mademoiselle*, this is no indication of the story's quality. Indeed, the story won an O. Henry Award in 1955.

"The City of the Living" is a very complex, rich, and moving story that would seem to have been generated out of the very depths of its author's soul, out of a terror that he could not report directly even to his closest friends. The story seems to be able, like tragedy, to inspire pity and fear as we become aware along with Chapman of being surrounded by the omnipresent threat of fate, a fate that no amount of "insurance" could forestall. For, like Chapman, we also try to operate safely from behind a barrier of antiseptic—to push away the unfortunate, hold at arm's length those who are foreign to us, remove ourselves as far away as possible from untamed nature, and embrace only that which is clean, safe, familiar, sanitized, and brand-name approved.

The Last of the Stories and
a Preface to the Great Novels

One Nation, the Stegner book dealing with discrimination in America, came out just as he and his family were moving to Palo Alto, California, in 1945. Over the next two years, among other occupations, he served on the board of the local chapter of the American Civil Liberties Union and gave numerous speeches around the Bay Area about the problems of racial, ethnic, and religious intolerance. At Stanford he made plans for the creative writing program that he hoped to build in the years to come—plans that were a bit grandiose, he admitted, but why not aim high? As someone who as a student had witnessed the birthing of the creative writing program at Iowa, who was a veteran of the Harvard writing program and a Briggs Copeland fellow there (fellowships that brought in writers to teach writing), and a longtime staff member at the Bread Loaf Writers Conference, few people could have been more qualified to start a university writing program. And few teachers could have approached the job with more enthusiasm or with a better sense of what such a program should include to be successful.

Most of all, he wanted to fund a group of fellowships, feeling that unless he could give at least some of his students a year or two free of money worries, he would not be able to attract the kind of promising writers that would make the program a success. He also hoped for prizes for outstanding work, yearly publication of a book collecting the best stories to come out of the program, and financing for the appointment of guest teachers who would be among the most prominent practitioners of the short story. Finally, he hoped to raise money to furnish a suitable seminar room, a place where, beyond its formal use, the students could feel comfortable to come and relax and share ideas with their fellows. All of this was made possible, miraculously, through the good offices of the brother of the department chairman. He was a rich oilman who was a frustrated writer and when he heard about Stegner's plans he funded all of them—permanently.

Stegner ran the program from its start in 1946 to his retirement from Stanford in 1971. Along the way he would have some influence in producing some of the most prominent writers of fiction of our time, including Ernest Gaines, Larry McMurtry, Wendell Berry, Eugene Burdick, Tillie Olsen, Al Young, Edward Abbey, Pat Zelver, Robert Stone, Evan Connell, Ken Kesey, Al Young, and James Houston. Most of these were "Stegner Fellows," as the fellowships were called shortly after they were established.

At the same time as he ran the program, conducted the writing seminar, and taught courses in American literature, Stegner was pursuing his own writing career as best he could. From 1946 to 1950, he published one novel, *Second Growth* (1947), and seven short stories, and then the direction of his career changed as he dropped the novel form and concentrated on the short story for a decade. The impetus for this change was his discouragement over the tepid critical reception and modest sales of a book that he felt had been a major effort, *The Preacher and the Slave*, which was published in 1950 (later entitled *Joe Hill*). But as he wrote to his agents, this was only the most recent disappointment in what he had come to feel that except for *The Big Rock Candy Mountain* was a discouraging record of novel publication as a whole:

> I have got some critical attention for short stories, not very much for novels. Neither has made me a living. On the Montgomery [British World War II Field Marshal Bernard Law Montgomery] theory that a commander should reinforce success, I have only the short stories to reinforce. I am tempted to say the hell with writing any more novels.[25]

He did say the hell with it for nearly 10 years, and even then his return to the novel, with publication of *A Shooting Star* (1961), was not auspicious. As we shall see, the path to the great novels of his last period would be blazed by trial and error through a series of short stories, just as his earlier success with *The Big Rock Candy Mountain* had come after publication of several of his Saskatchewan stories.

There were a number of important stories published during the 1950s, including "The Blue-Winged Teal" (1950), "The Traveler" (1951), "The City of the Living" (1954), "Maiden in a Tower" (1954), "The Volunteer" (1956), "He Who Spits at the Sky" (1958), and "Genesis" (1959). But the path to the techniques of the last novels starts back in 1946 with the writing of "The Women on the Wall" and finds its culmination in a story that never did find magazine publication, "Field Guide to the Western Birds" (published in Stegner's first collection, *The City of the Living*, and in *New Short Novels*, at the same time in 1956). The essence of what changed in his fiction, a change that makes its earliest appearance in "Field Guide," was point of view.

The first step along the way came in the development of a character—the elderly, observer-writer figure that we have already seen in "The Women on the Wall," who vaguely resembled the author. (Palmer is older than Stegner was at the time of writing, he is not a professional writer, and he is far less skeptical and realistic.) With the evolution of this persona in the late novels, starting with Joe Allston in "Field Guide," and going on with Joe Allston in *All the Little Live Things* (1967) and *Spectator Bird* (1976), Lyman Ward in *Angle of Repose*, and finally Larry Morgan in *Crossing to Safety*, this central character becomes more and more like his creator. Larry and Molly Morgan are so much like Wallace and Mary Stegner that at book signings for *Crossing to Safety* readers wanted to know why Mary (who unlike Molly had never suffered from polio) was not wearing braces.

As similar as the characters may be to their real-life counterparts, it must be insisted that Joe Allston and the others *are* fictions. As Stegner has written,

> Writers are far more cunning than the credulous reader supposes. We are all practiced shape-shifters and ventriloquists; we can assume forms and speak in voices not our own. We all have to have in some degree what Keats called negative capability, the capacity to make ourselves at home in other skins.[26]

Commencing with "Field Guide," Stegner switched from his habitual third-person, limited-omniscient point of view to the use of a first-person narrator. In doing so, he was able to achieve a voice close to his own, yet fictional, which would convey a sense of truth and conviction that came not, in the earlier Saskatchewan stories and *The Big Rock Candy Mountain*, out of the telling of his own story, but rather out of the force of his personality and belief.

"Voice" as I use it here is perhaps best described by Albert J. Guerard in *The Triumph of the Novel: Dickens, Dostoevsky, Faulkner*:

> The concept is of a "personal voice" discoverable in the work of every truly original writer: a voice that is the intimate and often unconscious *expression of his temperament and unborrowed personality*, a voice that in its structures and rhythms reflects the way his mind moves, and reflects too the particular needs and resistances of his spirit. [My emphasis.][27]

Stegner's early stories and novels, except for subject matter, could have been written by any skillful author. They are often very well-written, but there is little that is distinctive about them—they lack that recognizable stamp of "personality" that marks the very best fiction.

The importance of "Field Guide to the Western Birds" is that in the identity of its narrator and in its first-person telling Stegner is able to move from personal history to ongoing experience and observation. For many writers the problem of running out of personal history and finding other subject matter can be a crisis in their careers, a problem that some never do address successfully after their first autobiographical novel or group of stories about growing up. What brought Stegner to this success was simply that all his life he had been a person who felt he was without place or history and much, if not nearly all, his fiction as well as nonfiction embodied a search for those things. Now, late in life, he obviously felt he had achieved them and was a placed person with history, a sense of place, and personal identity that he had largely established for himself. From that security he could look out at life and his surroundings and reflect and comment on them, even though out of his own sense of humility he might find himself with ambivalent feelings and only tentative conclusions. All of his late fiction seems to reflect a certain self-criticism, a concern for how prone to error in our relations with others we humans tend to be. At last he was secure in himself, but at the same time full of questions, a man who never left his experiences unexamined.

Each novel carried by the first-person narrators mentioned above has as its central concern an effort to understand and make a judgment about a major character in that work, a pattern prefigured prominently in "Field Guide to the Western Birds." As noted earlier, each of these narrators—Joe Allston, Lyman Ward, and Larry Morgan—finds himself in a position where he is not only unsure of precisely what judgment to make but unsure about his own ability or qualifications to make that judgment. The one thing above all that these narrators try to avoid is thinking in terms of stereotypes, having their minds channeled by the cliché. The "dialogue," to use Bakhtin's term, in "Field Guide" and the novels is primarily concerned with a conflict between the narrator and one or more other characters about the nature or role of the ambiguous character who is both part of the discussion and the object of it.[28]

The Joe Allston of the story and the novels, even in his own time, was not a fashionable character—the late-middle-aged, white, upper-middle-class male in his sixties represented what was then referred to scornfully as "the establishment," and today has no credentials as an ethnic, racial, or gender victim to recommend him. Nevertheless, he seems to represent a point of view, a tone, an approach to life that is engaging, entertaining, and, above all, believable. The essence of the man that leads to our engagement is that he, like his creator, is a truth-seeker and a person extremely sensitive to the people around him and the dynamics of his physical environment. While Mr. Palmer in "The Women on the Wall" blunders into truth and is somewhat sorry for it, Joe Allston holds a stricter standard for himself and for others.

Like Palmer, he makes judgments and is proven wrong, but his judgments do not come out of his romantic illusions or his egotism, they come from better motives—out of his skeptical attempts to see behind appearances and his concern for the welfare of others. Unlike Mr. Palmer, Allston (and all his counterparts) is a learning character: Mr. Palmer is not going to modify his viewpoint or beliefs, but Allston, even at 66, is still wondering what the world is about and making judgments while wondering if he is right. Typically, not only in "Field Guide" but also in the novels, the narrator at any given moment may or may not be mistaken or wrongheaded. He isn't quite sure and neither are we, that is the beauty of it—life is ambiguous at best. Stegner's voice here provides ample opportunity for complex perceptions that can be variously interpreted. Stegner may have been scorned by some post-modernists as a "realist," but like Henry James or Edith Wharton his world is a rich mixture of complexities and ambiguities. In none of the stories by any of these authors do we, in the end, reach certainty.

The physical and social setting of "Field Guide to the Western Birds" is one patterned after Los Gatos Hills, a community behind Stanford where the Stegners built a home a few years after moving up from Santa Barbara. With its abundant trees, large brick patios, swimming pools, barbecues, and horses, it was a community that typified the image of California suburban living. In the late 1940s the area was rural, with almost no houses in the vicinity, but it developed into an upper-middle-class neighborhood where the Stegners could not possibly have afforded to buy into in recent years. As a modestly paid academic, Wallace really did not fit the mold of someone living in what Los Altos Hills became, although he and Mary did become friends with some of their wealthy neighbors. He was, in effect, both inside and outside the society that surrounded him, and that position, as reflected in the narrations of Joe Allston, made him the perfect observer.

Retired from a career as a literary agent in New York to a suburb on the San Francisco Peninsula, Joe Allston spends much of his time looking out his study window, bird watching, rather than writing his memoirs. This in itself is a complicated metaphor that stretches from the story into the two novels that also use him as narrator. First of all, of course, there is the declaration in the metaphor that this character is, above all, an observer. He looks out, away from himself, giving up the more self-involved occupation of writing memoirs, explaining with some irony at one point in the story, "I am beginning to understand the temptation to be literary and indulge the senses. It is a full-time job just watching and listening here" (*Collected Stories*, 313). Considering this from a biographical point of view, there would seem to be a subtext: Stegner for much of his career had been telling his personal history—in effect, writing his "memoirs"—and here he seems to be making a declaration that rather than dwelling on the past, he will now be looking outward and listening in the present.

Second, Joe's looking involves identification and classification, a process that extends from real birds to those "Western birds" or people that he encounters in his neighborhood and at social gatherings. At the party that takes up most of the story, he looks at the various guests and thinks, "It is all out of some bird book, how that species cling together, and the juncoes and the linnets and the seedeaters hop around in one place, and the robins raid the toyon berries *en masse*, and the jaybirds yak away together in the almond trees" (332). His story is a modified version of Mr. Palmer's story in that despite long experience with various kinds of people he learns, in the case of the guest of honor, that classifying people is not always as certain or as easy as classifying birds.

Joe and his wife, Ruth, have been invited by neighbors Bill and Sue Casement to a concert party—cocktails, a gourmet catered dinner, and after, outside near the pool, a recital by a down-on-his-luck young pianist, Kaminski. Kaminski turns out to be an arrogant and unhappy artist who does his best to insult everyone and to make Sue Casement, his benefactress, as uncomfortable as possible. At one point the pianist throws a tantrum about the guests eating and drinking so much before the performance. Standing in the buffet line, Joe and his wife see him stalk off, apparently threatening not to play, pursued by Sue, and Ruth comments:

> "If she weren't so nice it would be almost funny."
> "But she *is* so nice."
> "Yes," she says. "Poor Sue."

As I circle my nose above the heaped and delectable trencher, the thought of Kaminski's bald scorn of food and drink boils over my insides. Is he opposed to nourishment? "A pituitary monster," I say, "straight out of Dostoevsky."

"Your distaste was a little obvious."

"I can't help it. He curdled my adrenal glands."

"You make everything so endocrine," she says. He wasn't that bad. In fact, he had a point. It *is* a little alcoholic for a musicale."

"It's the only kind of party they know how to give."

"But it still isn't quite the best way to show off a pianist."

"All right," I say. "Suppose you're right. Is it his proper place to act as if he'd been captured and dragged here? He's the beneficiary, after all."

"I expect he has to humiliate her," Ruth says.

Sometimes she can surprise me. I remark that without an M.D. she is not entitled to practice psychiatry. So maybe he does have to humiliate her. That is exactly one of the seven thousand two hundred and fourteen things in him that irritate the hell out of me.

"But it'll be ghastly," says Ruth in her whisper, "if she can't manage to get him to play."

I address myself to the trencher. . . . But Ruth's remark of a minute before continues to go around in me like an auger, and I burst out again: "Humiliate her, uh? How to achieve power. . . . Did it ever strike you how much attention a difficult cross-grained bastard gets, just by being difficult?" (329–30)

Here, unlike some of the prose in his early novels, often so flat and uninspired, the dialogue crackles and snaps. One of the main things that Stegner achieves through this voice is interest. Joe—not to mention his wife—is intelligent, intensely observant, opinionated, and, above all, witty.

Although Joe, as we have just seen, takes an immediate dislike to this "Glandular Genius," as he calls Kaminski, he also begins to feel somewhat uncomfortable himself at the surfeit of food and drink on "this movie set where the standard of everything is excess" (334). The contradiction here to his objection to Kaminski saying pretty much the same thing underlines the ambiguity of Allston's position—he is both right and wrong in his reactions to the pianist. But there is also a foreshadowing in his feeling of discomfort at the surfeit of the party, a foreshadowing of the reversal of the ending, a hint that it is the condescension of the wealthy, as well-intentioned as they may be, toward the artist that is at the root of the conflict. It is a conflict that Joe feels but initially misunderstands. Another thing that Stegner achieves with the adoption of the Joe Allston voice is a narrator so complex in himself that the author is able to extend the dimensions of his narrative.

As the poolside performance begins, Joe listens carefully in order to hear how good a pianist Kaminski is, but typically, backtracks mentally, wondering if, after all, he is capable of any final judgment:

> God spare me from every being called a critic, or even a judge of music—even a listener. Like most people, I think I can tell a dub from a competent hand, and it is plain at once that Kaminski is competent. The shades of competence are another thing. They are where the Soul comes in, and I look with suspicion on those who wear their souls outside. I am not capable in any case of judging Kaminski's soul. Maybe it is such a soul as swoons into the world only once in a hundred years. Maybe, again, it is such a G. G. [Glandular Genius] soul as I have seen on Madison Avenue and elsewhere in my time. (336)

Later Allston almost gloats when he thinks he hears "a butch, a fat naked, staring discord" during Kaminski's performance of a difficult Bach piece (338). Here, as elsewhere throughout the story, Allston shows himself to be, if not expert, certainly very knowledgeable about music—once again contradicting himself and showing the difference between how he chooses to present himself to the reader—the modest appreciator of music—and the very acute critic he actually is. The reader, who by now shares Allston's dislike of Kaminski, is likely to want to celebrate the pianist's apparent incompetence and to find the pianist's disintegration after the recital almost predictable, almost enjoyable. In genteel terms, Kaminski turns out to be a thoroughly despicable case: in a long drunken public confession he proclaims his need to fail and his fraudulent identity as a Polish Jew victimized by the Nazis. Finally, when the host tries to pull him off to bed, he staggers into a chair and then falls into the pool. The harmony, the "niceness" as it might better be called in this upper-middle-class atmosphere, of the occasion has been thoroughly shattered.

But things are not as they seem. As Joe and Ruth drive home Joe discovers that Ruth, whose judgment in such matters he respects more than his own, thinks that Kaminski is, indeed, very good, exceptional—worth helping toward a concert in New York. But, of course, this chance, which might have been his only chance, is now gone. Joe wonders, "Why would he? . . . . Where in God's name does he belong?" and

How shall a nest of robins deal with a cuckoo chick? And how should a cuckoo chick, which has no natural home except the one he usurps, behave himself in a robin's nest? And what if the cuckoo is sensitive, or Spiritual, or insecure? Christ." (358)

The epiphany is ambiguous—the moral escapes him, and life remains as obscure as the fog that they drive through on the way back from the party. Joe can only be grateful to Ruth "for the forty years during which she has stood between me and myself" (339).

A complicated narrator—a fallible wise man, as he might be called—has led us down the garden path into a complex of emotions difficult for the reader to sort out. It is a pattern repeated over and over again in the final novels. Kaminski is brimming over with self-pity; he is a phony, a pretender; he is arrogant and cruel and filled with self-importance—so that Joe Allston's dislike, and ours, certainly seems justified. But Kaminski is also a poor Jewish young man of low self-esteem with a very real talent, thrust into a scene of upscale opulence dominated by a wealthy society that is with few exceptions largely populated by pretenders and Philistines—the entire party is a kind of charade of artistic appreciation. Isn't the artist's discomfort, posturing, and anger justified? Just because he makes a social stink, are we justified in hating him, gloating over his downfall? Just as in "Pop Goes the Alley Cat," we encounter the implicit question, how far can we stretch our empathy? Does it stretch only to those who model themselves after us, who look like us, who behave "nicely"? Despite his liberal inclinations and despite himself, Joe Allston has given us a demonstration of the workings of prejudice.

But even Joe Allston, who knows something about art and music, is wrong and comes to admit it, realizing that the identification of the human species can be a lot more difficult and fraught with possible error than he earlier in the story thinks it to be. At the end, the narrator is mired in doubt: "I don't know whether I'm tired, or sad, or confused. Or, maybe just irritated that they don't give you enough time in a single life to figure anything out" (359). If there is a lesson, it is not so much about the nature of life as it is about the processes of observing and judging others, a process that needs to be performed with humility and openness, with conclusions always subject to revision.

Such is the nature of this narrator as he evolved through the stories to become the voice, the fallible wise man of the late novels. Stegner has remarked that "[a]ny work of art is the product of a total human being,"[29] but it is only with these late works that he was able to bring himself totally to his art. The author is fond of quoting Robert Frost as saying that "a fiction writer should be able to tell what happened to himself as if it has happened to someone else, and what happened to someone else as if it had happened to himself" (*Teaching*, 24). At the beginning of his career, with such works as *On a Darkling Plain*, he tended to reverse Frost's admonition by telling what happened to someone else as if it did—giving distance to those things that were in fact distant.

Then, during his period of autobiographical fiction, in *The Big Rock Candy Mountain* and the stories that led up to it, he was able to make a correction, at least temporarily, bringing weight to his own story by giving it distance. But it is only with the evolution of the Joe Allston voice and stance that he was able to create a narrator that is a fiction, someone other than himself, yet bring to that fiction all his faculties, all the force of his personality. That which is distant—the fictional personality—is made near and real, and through the author's investment of himself, his deep participation, the complexities and ambiguities of living are made manifest.

The voices of Joe Allston and his counterparts make use of Wallace Stegner's personal assets—his dry sense of humor and wit; his willingness to laugh at himself and to examine himself; his skepticism; his openness to learning; his search for the truths behind cultural and historical myth; his concern for the preservation of the earth. Over time these narrators get closer and closer to the inner man, his concerns and values, as the man sheds his reluctance to risk and reveal himself. They are supercharged by the author's investment but remain fictions.

Written in 1952, "Field Guide to the Western Birds," as previously noted, was finally published in 1956 after considerable difficulty in placing it on the part of his agents. Two other stories set in the Los Gatos Hills area, "All the Little Live Things" and "Indoor-Outdoor Living," were also difficult to place, the latter finding publication as a last resort in a local journal, *Pacifica*. Several stories written in the 1950s, including "Garden Made for Snow," never did find publication despite the energetic efforts of his agents. All of this was, of course, considerably discouraging for a writer whose stories had previously had such success, appearing regularly in the *O. Henry* and *Best Short Stories* collections. It was even more depressing in that he had only a few years earlier made the decision to give up the novel and concentrate on short fiction. Now his career in that form, too, seemed to be going nowhere.

A good part of the reason for the difficulty in placing his stories was that the magazine market was changing, as several of the fiction editors reported to him with regret—what was taking over the women's magazines, even those like *Cosmopolitan* and *Redbook* that had a tradition of quality fiction, was romance, which was not Stegner's genre. And due to high publication costs and the need to increase advertising space, as well as the onset of television as a short-form entertainment medium, general magazines that published fiction were either beginning to disappear or were cutting back severely on the amount of fiction they were publishing. Although Stegner would write several more stories, including some of his best, such as "The Volunteer," "Genesis," and "The Wolfer," by 1958 he was almost through with the form and found that many of the ideas for stories, like "All the Little Live Things," were leading him to think of writing novels again. Later, as another reason for gradually giving up on the form, he would declare that short fiction was a young man's game: "It is made," he tells us, "for discoveries and nuances and epiphanies and superbly adapted for trial syntheses" (x). Many writers of fiction do indeed write most of their short works early in their careers. One reason Stegner had persisted with short stories as long as he did—he was over 50 when he stopped writing them—was that he was interested in the form itself and was constantly involved in teaching it.

Of course his career as writer of fiction did not end with his giving up the short form. Largely as a result of the voice that he had crafted in his stories of the 1940s and 1950s, he would go on to win the Pulitzer Prize for fiction for *Angle of Repose* in 1972 and the National Book Award for fiction for *The Spectator Bird* in 1977. His last novel, also employing a variation of that voice in the narrator Larry Morgan, was the best-selling *Crossing to Safety* (1987), an amazing success story considering it was, in the Stegner tradition, a quiet story of human nature that lacked completely the sensational elements of subject that typically make a best-selling novel.

Toward the end of his life, the *Collected Stories* was published in 1990. In her review of the collection in the *New York Times Book Review*, Anne Tyler wrote that even though, as Stegner tells us in his foreword, he had given up the form some years earlier,

> his admirers will take him any way they can get him—novels, essays, biographies—but after sinking into these stories gathered from "a lifetime of writing," we can't help but mourn the passing of his short story

days. These stories are so large; they're so wholehearted. Plainly, he never set out to write a *mere* short story. It was all or nothing.[29]

On April 12, 1993, Wallace Stegner died of injuries sustained in an auto accident in Santa Fe, New Mexico, where he had traveled to accept an award from the Montana and Plains Booksellers Association.

Notes to Part I

1. Wallace Stegner, *Where the Bluebird Sings to the Lemonade Springs: Living and Writing in the West* (New York: Random House, 1992), 30. Hereafter cited in the text as *Bluebird*.

2. *Collected Stories of Wallace Stegner* (New York: Random House, 1990), 13. All further references to the short stories in part I are from this volume and are cited in the text as *Collected Storie* in parenthesis following the quotation.

3. Don Kazak, "What Wallace Writes," *Palo Alto Weekly*, May 2, 1990, 29. Hereafter cited in the text.

4. Wallace Stegner, *Wolf Willow* (New York: The Viking Press, 1962), 134, 136. Hereafter cited in the text.

5. Wallace Stegner, Foreword to *My Dear Wister: The Frederic Remington-Owen Wister Letters*, by Ben Merchant Vorpahl, as reprinted in Wallace Stegner, *One Way to Spell Man* (Garden City, N.Y.: Doubleday & Company, Inc, 1982), 109.

6. Wallace Stegner, "Variations on a Theme by Crevecoeur," in *Bluebird*, 107.

7. Wallace Stegner, "Autobiography: Wallace Stegner," in *Contemporary Authors: Autobiography Series* (Detroit: Gale Research Company, 1989), 9:261.

8. Wallace Stegner, interview, July 20, 1987.

9. Wallace Stegner, "Robert Frost: A Lovers Quarrel with the World," *Stanford Today* 133 (1961): n. pag. Hereafter cited in the text as "Robert Frost."

10. Wallace Stegner, "Growing Up Western," ts., Stegner papers, n.pag.

11. Wallace Stegner with Richard Etulain, *Conversations with Wallace Stegner about Western Literature and History* (Salt Lake City: University of Utah Press, 1983), 25.

12. Wallace Stegner, "Born a Square," in *The Sound of Mountain Water* (Garden City, N.Y.: Doubleday & Company, Inc., 1969), 179.

13. Milton Cowan, interview, April 4, 1986.

14. "Autobiography," ts., Stegner papers, 18, Marriott Library Special Collections, University of Utah.

15. Nancy Packer, interview, March 6, 1987.

16. Israel Shenker, "Whither the short story?", *New York Times*, November 20, 1970, n.pag. Hereafter cited in the text.

17. Wallace Stegner, "The Twilight of Self-Reliance: Frontier Values and Contemporary America," in *The Tanner Lectures on Human Values*, ed. Sterling M. McMurrin (Salt Lake City: University of Utah Press, 1981), 221.

18. Julie Kirgo, "The Healing Country," *Vermont Magazine* (January/February 1993): 60.

19. Robert Frost, *Complete Poems of Robert Frost* (New York: Henry Holt and Company, 1959), 19. Hereafter cited in the text as *Complete Poems*.

20. Wallace Stegner, Letter to Phil and Peg Gray, October 14, 1942.

21. Stephen Crane, "The Open Boat," in *The Red Badge of Courage and Selected Prose and Poetry*, ed. William M. Gibson (New York: Rinehart & Co, Inc., 1956), 88.

22. Wendell Berry as quoted by Wallace Stegner, "The Sense of Place," in *Bluebird*, 199.

23. Wallace Stegner "A Problem in Fiction," *The Pacific Spectator* 3 (1949): 370. Hereafter cited in the text as "Problem."

24. Wallace Stegner, Letter to Phil and Peg Gray, November 6, 1950.

25. Wallace Stegner, Letter to agents, Brandt and Brandt, September 17, 1951.

26. Wallace Stegner, "The Law of Nature and the Dream of Man: Ruminations on the Art of Fiction," *Bluebird*, 217.

27. Albert J. Guerard, *The Triumph of the Novel: Dickens, Dostoevsky, Faulkner* (New York: Oxford University Press, 1976), 136.

28. Mikhail Bakhtin, *Problems of Dostoevsky's Poetics*, trans. Caryl Emerson (Minneapolis: University of Minnesota Press, 1984), 4.

29. Wallace Stegner, *On the Teaching of Creative Writing*, ed. Connery Lathem (Hanover, N.H.: University Press of New England, 1988), 22. Hereafter cited in the text as *Teaching*.

30. Anne Tyler, "The Outsider May Be You," *The New York Times Book Review*, March 18, 1990, 2.

Part 2

THE WRITER

Introduction: Wallace Stegner
as Teacher and Practitioner

Wallace Stegner wrote so much about writing and teaching the writing of the short story, that it is difficult to select what should be included here. However, I have quoted from some of these essays in Part 1, and a complete list of his writings on the subject is included in the bibliography near the end of this volume under "Primary Works," and the reader is invited to sample Stegner's discussions of these and related subjects further.

What I have chosen to include here are items of three different kinds. The first is not an article by Stegner, but a newspaper account of a reading and informal speech he gave during a signing of his *Collected Stories* shortly after publication in 1990 at a Menlo Park, California, bookstore. This may seem an unusual inclusion, but it does give, first of all, a very definite sense of the man in person. Second, the article quotes liberally from Stegner's remarks regarding his views of the short story form and an account of his writing regimen. Third, in the article Stegner is quoted discussing his composition of one particular short story, "The Traveler," before reading it to his audience.

The second item in Part 2 is a short essay, "Fiction: A Lens on Life," which gives us Stegner's general philosophy of what fiction is or should be, and his conception of the role of the fiction writer as artist. Drawing the distinction between the writer of serious fiction and the writer of escape entertainment, he goes on to declare that "it is the job of [the] serious artist to bring order where no order was before him." While the writer of entertainment may do a workmanlike job of applying a formula, the writer as artist will find every piece of fiction "a trial of [his] whole understanding and a reflection of his whole feeling and knowing." Thus writing fiction, long or short, was for Stegner a serious business. Elsewhere, in several places, he has declared that writing fiction should be an expression of belief, certainly not self-expression, which he equated with self-indulgence.

The third item, "A Problem in Fiction," is very specific. It is highly unusual in that it traces, step by step, the thought processes and composition of a single short story, "The Women on the Wall." I don't know of a similar essay anywhere (although Henry James wrote about his own composition, he did so usually only briefly, long after the fact, and in rather general terms). Although I have quoted from this essay in my discussion of the story in Part 1, the entire essay in all its details should be of interest to the reader.

What Wallace Writes

A half hour before Wallace Stegner was scheduled to begin reading at Kepler's Books & Magazines in Menlo Park last Wednesday night, the store was jammed with his fans to the point where aisles were impassable. The 125 folding chairs had been long occupied, while at least that many people again peered over bookshelves and from other vantage points.

The occasion was the publication of *The Collected Stories of Wallace Stegner,* 31 of his stories that had initially been published in magazines and small reviews and in two previous collections. There wasn't a story in the batch less than 30 years old. As Stegner later put it, since 1960 or so, "everything I wanted to write somehow wanted to be long." While there may not have been any new stories, a new publication by Stegner is still an event of some note around here, hence the standing-room-only crowd that jammed Kepler's.

A lot of people purchased the new collection, while others brought their Stegner favorites for autographs—the Pulitzer-Prize-winning *Angle of Repose*, the National-Book-Award-winning *The Spectator Bird*, or, his most recent novel, *Crossing to Safety*. The author of 13 novels and 11 volumes of essays and non-fiction, Stegner is as well known as a teacher of writers as a writer, founding the creative writing program at Stanford shortly after World War II.

"I don't have any formula or theory of the short story," he said before he began reading. "The only thing I do demand of a short story, my own or anyone else's, is that it ought to close some sort of circuit—a plot circuit, an emotional circuit, psychological circuit, a circuit of understanding, so in the end there is some sense of completion." Stegner said his stories somehow reflected his own experiences, "reasonably closely, but not accurately."

This article by Don Kazak is reprinted with permission from the *Palo Alto (California) Weekly*, May 2, 1990. Copyright © 1990 Embarcadero Publishing Co.

As an example, the story he read was "The Traveler," the story of a medicine supply salesman whose car breaks down on a harsh winter night out in the country. The salesman, who sets out to find help, later must be the one to give help when he encounters a boy whose grandfather has fallen ill. But the story came out of his own experience when he was on a skiing trip in Vermont. "It was about 20 below, everyone had the flu, the car wouldn't start, and I had to walk about two miles to town in a magical kind of moonlight to get some help," he said. When he returned, he found that his own temperature was back to normal—he had "walked off" his fever.

The moonlight walk reminded Stegner of his own childhood in Saskatchewan, Canada. "The lights in an arctic night, the stars and the moon, the lights of the heavens, are pretty magical," he said. So a walk in the winter's countryside as a young professor reminded him of his childhood, and somehow that got translated into a fictional story of a salesman whose car broke down. "Don't trust the details," he explained, "trust the feeling."

Stegner said that his stories "are places where I have paused more or less to understand something that happened." A surprising example of that is his most recent novel, *Crossing to Safety*. "I didn't write *Crossing to Safety* as a novel," he said, but "as a memoir. I was just trying to get some friends of ours down where I could understand them. It turned out to be a novel because I invented a whole lot more than I intended. I was going to do that one right straight from life, but I can't do that. I'm not to be trusted with life; I keep inventing it."

Noting that he "has no gift for the kinds of magic realism or fantasy or other things that are popular at the moment," Stegner said, "you can't really go out and commit experience in order to write about it. You have to take it after it has happened to you and make some sense of it. Henry James said once if you have to make notes on how something has struck you, it probably hasn't struck you. On the other hand, it has to be analyzed before you can make fiction out of it."

In his book *On the Teaching of Creative Writing*, Stegner wrote: "Robert Frost used to say that a fiction writer should be able to tell what happened to himself as if it had happened to someone else, and what happened to someone else as if it had happened to himself. That puts the emphasis where it belongs: on the technique of communication, the persuasiveness of the fiction." Stegner's own technique is to write every morning when working on a novel, working solidly from breakfast to lunch. "I hardly ever do a first draft because I'm always rewriting. This is why people tell me I should get a computer, but I haven't."

In the question and answer period following his reading, Stegner was asked which of his books was the most fun to write, and which were his favorites. "The fact is I don't enjoy writing many of them," he replied, "they're work. It's awfully nice when it clicks, and if it comes out reasonably well, there's a satisfaction in it which is more fun than fun, really." What Stegner does like is rewriting a draft, "because you've already got to the end and you know how it comes out, and all you have to do is clean it up."

Stegner's favorites of his own works include *Angle of Repose, The Spectator Bird, Crossing to Safety,* and "although I wrote it before I knew how," *The Big Rock Candy Mountain,* published in 1943. Stegner, patient, unpretentious ("you can ask me anything") and plain-talking, did his best to answer in detail all the questions he was asked. Afterwards, he was stationed at a small table for more than an hour, unhurriedly autographing copies of his various books for his fans.

Fiction: A Lens on Life

The editor of a mass-circulation magazine once told me proudly that all through the Depression he had published not one story dealing with the Depression's peculiar problems. No unemployment, no flophouses, no breadlines, no despair. Nonfiction articles by the dozen dealt with these things, but stories and serials, no. Fiction was for fun, not for illumination. Fiction was phenobarbital, not amphetamine. And even "quality" magazines, which presumably have other views of fiction, are not entirely uninfluenced by considerations of escape. I have known such a magazine, one of the best published in the United States, to refuse a story that every editor on the staff was enthusiastic about, and to refuse it only because it dealt with a woman dying of cancer. The magazine's audience contained a good many elderly women, and fiction should not touch their fears.

The kind of fiction which, approvingly or otherwise, may be called lies is outside the present discussion. It is fiction as truth that I am concerned with here, fiction that reflects experience instead of escaping it, that stimulates instead of deadening. Serious fiction, so called, is written by a different kind of writer and for a different audience. It differs in intention, in materials, in method, and in its final effect. If it entertains—as it must—it entertains at a higher intellectual and emotional level; if it deals in make-believe—as it likewise must—it creates a make-believe world in order to comment on the real one. Serious fiction is not necessarily great and not even necessarily literature, because the talents of its practitioners may not be as dependable as their intentions. But all literature, including the great, will be written in this spirit.

The difference between the writer of serious fiction and the writer of escape entertainment is the clear difference between the artist and the craftsman. The one has the privilege and the faculty of original design; the other does not. The man who works from blueprints is a thoroughly

This article by Wallace Stegner originally appeared in *The Saturday Review*, April 22, 1950, and was reprinted in *One Way to Spell Man*. It is reprinted here by permission of Mary Page Stegner.

respectable character, but he is of another order from the man who makes the blueprints in the first place.

The word "artist" is not a word I like. It has been adopted by crackpots and abused by pretenders and debased by people with talent but no humility. In its capital-A form it is the hallmark of that peculiarly repulsive sin of arrogance by which some practitioners of the arts retaliate for public neglect or compensate for personal inadequacy. I use it here only because there is no other word for the serious "maker" in words or stone or sound or colors.

Joseph Conrad once outlined the qualifications for the serious artist in a little essay called simply "Books." He said:

> A novelist who would think himself of a superior essence to other men would miss the first condition of his calling. To have the gift of words is no such great matter. A man furnished with a long-range weapon does not become a hunter or a warrior by the mere possession of a firearm; many other qualities of character and temperament are necessary to make him either one or the other. Of him from whose armory of phrases one in a hundred thousand may perhaps hit the far-distant and elusive mark of art I would ask that in his dealings with mankind he should be capable of giving a tender recognition to their obscure virtues. I would not have him impatient with their small failings and scornful of their errors. I would not have him expect too much gratitude from that humanity whose fate, as illustrated in individuals, it is open to him to depict as ridiculous or terrible. I would wish him to look with a large forgiveness at men's ideas and prejudices, which are by no means the outcome of malevolence, but depend on their education, their social status, even their professions. . . . I would wish him to enlarge his sympathies by patient and loving observation while he grows in mental power. It is in the impartial practice of life, if anywhere, that the promise of perfection for his art can be found, rather than in the absurd formulas trying to prescribe this or that particular method of technique or conception. Let him mature the strength of his imagination among the things of this earth. . . .

It is the job of this serious artist to bring order where no order was before him or at least where his own special kind of order was not. He has for material the whole of his experience, actual and vicarious, and the wider and deeper it is, the better. The more it has hurt him, short of actual crippling, the better. The more he has enjoyed it, the better. But this experience by which he estimates the experience of men at large is always disorderly and contradictory and in our times is apt to be an utter chaos. What he does to it is to shape it in patterns of words that are idea and image and character. Somewhere in the morass of his world he tramples out a foothold, or, to change the figure, he bounds the panoramic and bewildering view with his squared hands. The most inclusive vision is not necessarily his aim; it is the *clearest* vision he is after, and this may involve squinting or shutting one eye or even bending over and looking at the view upside down through his spraddled legs, Japanese fashion. However he does it—and his method is his own business—he tries with every piece of fiction, even the slightest short story, to "create a world." The phrase is Conrad's, the job is the endlessly repeated and endlessly new job of every serious writer. Every piece of fiction is thus not the application of a formula, not a neat and workmanlike job of joining and fitting, not an exercise in cleverness, but a trial of the writer's whole understanding and a reflection of his whole feeling and knowing.

Because he writes fiction in order to reflect or illuminate life, his materials obviously must come out of life. These materials are people, places, things—especially people. If fiction isn't people it is nothing, and so any fiction writer is obligated to be to some degree a lover of his fellowmen, though he may, like the Mormon preacher, love some of them a damn sight better than others. The people of his stories and novels will be, inevitably but in altered shapes, the people he himself has known. The flimsy little protestations that mark the front gate of every novel, the solemn statements that any resemblance to real persons living or dead is entirely coincidental, are fraudulent every time. A writer has no other material to make his people from than the people of his experience. If there is no resemblance to any real person, living or dead, the character is going to be pretty unconvincing. The only thing the writer can do is to recombine parts, suppress some characteristics and emphasize others, put two or three people into one fictional character, and pray the real-life prototypes won't sue.

The fiction writer is an incorrigible lover of concrete *things*. He has to build fiction out of such materials as the hard knotting of anger in the solar plexus, the hollowness of a night street, the sound of poplar leaves. In a contentious preface to a World War II Italian novel, Ernest Hemingway put it for the whole tribe:

> A writer finds rain [by which he means reality] to be made of knowledge, experience, wine, bread, oil, salt, vinegar, bed, early mornings, nights, days, the sea, men, women, dogs, beloved motor cars, bicycles,

hills and valleys, the appearance and disappearance of trains on straight and curved tracks ... cock grouse drumming on a basswood log, the smell of sweet grass and fresh smoked leather and Sicily.

By his very profession, a serious fiction writer is a vendor of the sensuous particulars of life, a perceiver and handler of things. His most valuable tools are his senses and his memory; what happens in his mind is primarily pictures. He is not ordinarily or ideally a generalizer, not a dealer in concepts, though some writers have tried to intellectualize fiction in this way under the impression that they were making it more respectable.

Ideas, of course, have a place in fiction, and any writer of fiction needs a mind. But ideas are not the best *subject matter* for fiction. They do not dramatize well. They are, rather, a by-product, something the reader himself is led to formulate after watching the story unfold. The ideas, the generalizations, ought to be implicit in the selection and arrangement of the people and places and actions. They ought to haunt a piece of fiction as a ghost flits past an attic window after dark.

Any good serious fiction is collected out of reality, and its parts ought to be vivid and true to fact and to observation. The parts are reassembled in such a way that the architecture, the shape of the action, is meaningful. And if the fiction is good enough, that meaning will stretch, the building will throw a shadow longer than itself, the particular will become representative, general, symbolic, indefinitely applicable to other people, other situations. The writer's meaning is thus not a single or inert thing. It expands, it becomes part of the living thought of its readers. And it is this capacity for generalized meaning that gives serious fiction its illuminating and liberating effect. But no fiction should be asked to state its meaning flatly, in conceptual terms, any more than a ghost should be called upon to come out and stand a physical examination.

The methods a writer uses to arrive at this kind of meaning are relatively unimportant except to himself. Different writers will always get their foothold in reality in different ways, different places. Every generation finds its own way of speaking out, says Gertrude Stein. No classic looks anything like any classic that has preceded it, says Hemingway. The important writer will be recognizable not by new materials but by new insights, says V. S. Pritchett.

It is often necessary for a writer to distort the particulars of experience in order to see them better. As was remarked earlier, he can look upside down or squint or put on gauze spectacles or do what he chooses, so long as his method lets him see at least part of his world more clearly. To take only one example, the padded nightmare world of Franz Kafka represents a new insight. The solemnly logical course of the incredible begets a new satire and a new humor and for all its strangeness Kafka's fiction reflects real men and real institutions better than many more-representational kinds of fiction.

Whatever the method, it will involve a simplification. By inexorable necessity, all art simplifies. Hemingway, learning to write "beginning with the simplest things," stripping his vocabulary to the bare Anglo-Saxon, reducing his sentences to the simple declarative, eliminating all latinate complexity, and trying to eliminate even such customary "cheating" as metaphor, simplifying his people and simplifying his themes, peeling down even his favorite theme of death to its simplest and most violent forms, represents only one kind, an extreme kind, of artistic simplification. The world that results in Hemingway's fiction may not be a world we like, but it is unmistakably a world. Conrad's world, in its own way, is just as simplified. Often it is a world within one ship, its deck the whole earth and its crew all mankind, and the moral universe bending over the actions of his people as close or as remote as the stars at sea. Even Henry James, on the surface one of the most complex and hairsplitting and qualifying and entangled of fictionists, begins with absolutely sweeping simplifications. To clear the way for the unimpeded moral choices which form the crucial moments of all his stories, he first eliminates most of what some other novelists might build their whole books from. No James character ever has to worry about making a living; James endows them all with handy inheritances. No James character is fettered by family responsibilities or any of the complex nets that fasten about the feet of people in life. All of James's people are free to move at will through the world he has made for them, absolutely and deliberately set free from all mundane entanglements so that their moral choices can be "pure" and uninfluenced. And though the complexities of the actual choice, the backing and filling, the delicate hesitancies and withholdings, the partial renunciations and the hair-fine scruples, may be almost maddeningly complex, the act of simplification which has made this complexity possible is just as impressive.

Any simplification the artist chooses is legitimate; it can be judged only on pragmatic grounds, by its success. Every writer is a blind man feeling the elephant, and even a great writer is likely to be limited in what he understands. His fictional world will reflect the special understandings he has. The world of Chekhov, in which unhappy people walk gray, muddy roads or ferry exiles like themselves across leaden Siberian rivers or take a moment's wry enjoyment from a wistful and frustrated life, is valid and recognizable; so is the world Tom Lea creates in *The Brave Bulls*, where man's confrontation of the immortal Terror takes the shape of the ritualized spectacle of a bullfight. In *The Sheltering Sky*, Paul Bowles obtains his essential simplification by an act of arbitrary violence, putting down a pair of New York sophisticates in the primitive Sahara. The act is precisely like the act of putting a smear of culture on a slide for inspection under the microscope.

Certainly no writer can see or know all or get all life into his fiction. His quality will be measured by the amount he does succeed in getting without blurring the edges of his simplifying frame. It is the frame, the limitation, that produces for the reader the limited field of vision that can be seen under an intense light and in sharpened focus.

The effect of reading fiction conceived and executed on such terms should be an enlarged understanding. But one element of this enlarged understanding which is too often overlooked is something I can call only "intense acquaintance." In all our wandering through real or fictional worlds it is probably ourselves we seek, and since that encounter is impossible we want the next-best thing: the completely intimate contact which may show us another like ourselves. I am willing if necessary to risk condemnation as an advocate of what C. S. Lewis has called the "personal heresy," though it is certainly no such biographical hunger as Mr. Lewis deplores that I speak of here. It is utterly irrelevant that Milton misused his daughters or that Conrad had a habit of flipping bread pellets around the dinner table. What is relevant is the artist himself, or his refined and distilled spirit, the totality of his understanding. Acquaintance on that level is a thing found very rarely in life, but a book which has profoundly and intensely moved us is a most intimate experience, perhaps more intimate than marriage and more revealing than fifty years of friendship. We can make closer contact in fiction than in reality; more surely than we know the secrets of our friends, we know how this writer who is something like ourselves looks upon himself, how he fronts his life, how he, another waif in a bewildering world, has made out to survive and perhaps be at peace.

Ultimately, I am convinced, he is what we read for. The work of art is not a gem, as some schools of criticism would insist, but truly a lens. We look through it for the purified and honestly offered spirit of the artist. The ghosts of meaning that flit past the window of his fictional house wear his face. And the reward of a lifetime of reading is a rich acquaintanceship with those gentle or powerful or rebellious or acceptant, those greatly mixed and humanly various but always greatly human ghosts.

A Problem in Fiction

There are so many kinds of stories that one cannot hope, by analyzing or re-creating one, to say anything very definitive about the form. One kind, intensely personal in feeling, deriving often from memory, its origins clouded and obscured by time, its methods so unconscious and undeliberate that the story seems to grow by itself out of some fecund darkness, can reward analysis only if the analysis searches out the whole mental and emotional state of the author during composition, and becomes a kind of personality analysis, a study in Jungian terms of the creative process and the creative personality. Another kind, built deliberately according to predetermined blueprints, is hardly worth analysis no matter how skillfully it is made, because the skill is all it has; it exists at a rudimentary level, without the difficult and indispensable quality of original design. It is the quality of design which I assume we are after in this series of story re-creations, and what may be valuable in such a study is the simple record of how a story came into being, how the scattered materials of time and place and people and situation and idea and feeling and significant action were subjected to some sort of synthesis and emerged a new thing, with a form of its own.

Almost any professional writer has had stories write themselves for him. I suppose most of us look upon that kind of story with a slight awe: it comes so easily and it leaves no tracks. Almost any writer too has had on occasion to build a story from scanty suggestions or fragmentary experiences, to hew one out by main force. This latter kind lends itself better to critical retrospection because its processes, if not exactly clear, have been at least painful.

"The Women on the Wall" is a story that had to be hewn out. It is one of the few I ever wrote directly from a scene and a group of people immediately under my eyes, and perhaps because I knew nothing about any of these people except their external appearance and their general

This article by Wallace Stegner originally appeared in the 1949 issue of *The Pacific Spectator* as the third in a series of articles on story writing. It is reprinted here with permission of Mary Page Stegner.

situation, and so was without the help of the gestative processes which memory and the subconscious often perform painlessly, I had a good deal of difficulty in finding out exactly what my story was *about*. Action is an easy thing to invent and a hard thing to guide, because to guide it you must know where you want it to go.

Since I am engaged in a process of re-creation, let me re-create. The circumstances which gave rise to the story were not in any way unusual; the idea began casually and accidentally, in the middle of a time of let-down and boredom. I had returned to Santa Barbara from New York in the spring of 1945 to recover from an illness and a long stretch of working on racial minorities in the United States. I was in that state of mild collapse that follows the finishing of a book. Habit drove me to my desk after breakfast, but I could think of nothing I really wanted to do there. I wrote letters, or looked out the window across a lovely pine-shrouded point and a sunken lane, with the Pacific shining beyond and the mornings so still and temperate that I almost felt the house wallow slightly, like a ship in a dead calm. I smelled the slow warm fume of that little promontory—pine and eucalyptus and wood smoke and Ceanothus and kelp, and heard the relaxed swash of surf on the beach.

And I saw the Army and Navy wives who lived in apartments in the old beach club building on the point. Every morning about eleven they began to gather on the stone wall at the end of the lane, and for a half-hour, three-quarters, an hour, sometimes longer, they waited as quietly as patients sunning themselves in a sanitarium garden, until the mailman in his gray car and gray uniform drove up to the row of mailboxes.

Perhaps the way that picture formed and broke up every noon, only to re-form again in almost identical shapes and colors the next day, impressed it upon me unduly. Perhaps the women did not have over them the still purity of light that I thought I saw. Nevertheless I saw them waiting there under an intense stillness, a picture of a wistful charm. Before two mornings had passed, what I really did in my study was watch that most beautiful, lulled, enchanted place above the blue and violet sea, with the frieze of bright, still women along the wall.

I have no idea at what point I began to think of them as a story. It was simply apparent after awhile that I felt them with the clarity and force of a symbol, and that I wanted to write them. But you do not write a picture. You do not even write a "situation" like this of the women waiting patiently at the remote edge of the West while their husbands fought the Japanese thousands of miles westward across that miraculous water.

Waiting was obviously a significant wartime activity, but it was fairly inert stuff to make a story from.

The women waited, as women have always waited in wars, and I watched them as avidly as a Peeping Tom. I saw how they were tuned-down, stilled, withdrawn into themselves until they seemed to have little to say even to each other. I heard the surf on the beach below, and the surf was slow and muted. I saw the mornings pass over as even and imperturbable as the muted sea and the waiting women. I knew that these images and shapes of quiescence that came to me might sometime be useful, that they were the images from which an atmosphere could be created, but I did not see any story around which to create an atmosphere. The images lay around in my mind at random, unconnected, and though I must even in the beginning have had some perception of how everything that struck me as important about those women had a cyclic, reiterative compulsiveness—tides and waves and growing mornings and the gathering along the wall and the climactic and awaited coming of the gray car—I was too interested in the images singly to see their significance en masse.

And another confession of almost unbelievable obtuseness: I had watched the women for upwards of a week, and been reminded of Keats's "On a Grecian Urn" a dozen times, and been impressed every morning freshly by the clear Attic light, the Mediterranean clarity, of the picture the women made. But it was a week before I made the connection with Penelope on the rocky isle of Ithaca above the wine-dark sea waiting her twenty years for Ulysses' return.

That belated perception of the classical parallel took me forward a long step. The very roll and ring of Homer's epithets and the soft thunder of his names added a dimension, dignity, depth. So I found myself with a place, a group of people, a situation, a classical parallel that had the effect of a stereopticon viewer. But I still had no story. I still had only a picture.

I attempted to surprise a story out of the picture by simply beginning, describing the point and the light and the sound of surf and the incense smells and the graceful waiting women. But when I got the picture finished everything stopped. And every attempt I made to invent and import some action fell flat. The Penelope parallel tempted me into inventing suitors, but they were as out of place in what I had already half-conceived as Keystone cops would have been. I was tempted by the communal, enforced life the women led in the beach club to try a kind of Grand Hotel scheme, following each woman and each woman's husband to a conclusion, whether death or reunion or separation or misunderstanding. But everything I tried was off key, or involved complication enough for a novel. And I kept being pulled back to the picture, just that. After several false starts and ten days of watching, certain things began to be clear.

It was clear that these women fascinated me precisely because they did nothing but wait. The minute I started them acting I falsified them. Their proper story was not a story, but only a repetition, and the conflict proper to their lives was only the tugging on the chain that held them. Waiting itself was their essential struggle. They were all thrown out of their normal posture by the war; they lived suspended lives.

It was clear too that if I wanted to dramatize that suspension properly, the method must be repetitive. That much I might borrow from the Grand Hotel theme; the effects of waiting must be seen in more than one way and in more than one of the women. And since the conflict here was internal, the story would probably resolve itself down not into a clear line of action, but into a series of uncoverings, all set within the framework of the daily waiting for the mail. The problem, I finally began to see, was not to make action out of this picture, but by moving the picture slightly to reveal what was hidden behind it. This story would develop, certainly, not as a complication resolved but as what Henry James called a "situation revealed."

And if revealed, it must be revealed to someone. I had already tried, with a dismal sense of failure, to get at these women from the inside. In the end I adopted the point of view that was at once easiest and most natural—my own, the viewpoint of the external observer. I elected to make my observer a man, for no particular reason; I made him an older man to prevent any suggestion of his being interested in the women for the wrong reasons, and to avoid the necessity of explaining how a young man could be on this secluded bit of beach during wartime. In the end I decided that he had just recently returned from many years on the Galapagos Islands, because as a retired colonial he might be assumed to have a certain innocence, because he would have along with that innocence an interest in rediscovering things in the States, because he could first be impressed and then shocked or startled at the uncoverings I was intending to make. I set his earlier career on the Galapagos only because every night at that time I was playing a game called "Cargoes" with my son, and almost every night I stopped my marker at the Galapagos for a cargo of turtles.

My story will still not clear to me in detail, but by now I knew what I thought. I thought the waiting women were lovely and symbolic and touching; and I thought that their quiet could not possibly be more than skin-deep, that beneath their muted surface must be a seethe and dart of emotion like a school of small fish just under the unbroken surface of water. I suspected, though I didn't know and don't know yet, that their submission was only apparent and that they were all ready to explode with anger, hysterics, loss, boredom, fear.

Though I certainly did not formulate the notion to myself as I started to write, I had a pattern of reversal all prepared for myself. Whether it is a complication resolved or a situation revealed, fiction normally works either toward surprise or toward recognition. Whichever it works toward, it covers its tracks, it moves by stealth, it pretends to be going the other way. Like a lever, a story needs a fulcrum of opposition on which to get what we used to call "purchase." If boy is going to get girl, it usually is rigged so that for most of the story he apparently is going to lose her, and vice versa. So in this story, since the uncoverings were going to reveal unsuspected depths of passion and resentment and resistance in these women, I began with what had been my own first impression: the enchanted point, the breathing sea, the cyclic mornings and tides and mailman, the quiet cataleptic pattern of the women on the wall, the apparent submission to their waiting.

By now I had to know more about my characters than their external appearance. Quite without their consent or knowledge, I gave to one of them, Mrs. Kendall, an adopted child, a warped and bottled-up and prudish interest in sex, and a personal inadequacy matched by her personal loneliness; I gave another an illegitimate unborn child whose father rarely wrote and was constantly in danger of death; to another I gave defiance and a corrective hostility against those outside her own life; to a fourth I gave an intense and nervous temperament, the habit of smoking marijuana, and a husband who preferred combat to his home. I had my Mrs. Corson smoke marijuana rather than punish highballs because I had recently been working with Mexican youths in Los Angeles and I had marijuana on my mind. So much of what attaches itself or insinuates itself when one is making a story is purest accident; the story growing in the mind becomes a kind of flypaper that catches everything light, everything loose.

The form the story was taking was organic; it could not be separated from the materials, it took on definiteness as the materials clarified themselves. All I had to do was to start my Mr. Palmer where I had started, have him see and admire the women, respect their withdrawal, idealize them as Penelopes, be impressed with the classic purity of their situation. I did this. I allowed Mr. Palmer to try making their acquaintance and I let him be rebuffed, and I had him apologize to himself for their behavior. They were heroically doing what they had to do; they should not be intruded upon. He went back to his role as respectful observer.

Now I needed an incident to bring him close to them again, so that from a certain point on he could become progressively more aware of the seething under the quiet surface. Fate provided me the incident in the form of an unexplained cocker pup who appeared for one whole day in the beach club yard, howled and yipped and mourned for twelve hours, and mysteriously disappeared again. I incorporated him and his adventure bodily, using him not only as a means of characterizing Mrs. Kendall, but also as a symbolic representation *in petto* of the way everybody in the story, adult, child, or dog, was tied down helplessly and no relief for it.

Having brought Mr. Palmer into contact with one of the women, Mrs. Corson, I was in shape to have her use him as a screen for one of her marijuana binges. On the pretext of going down to take her daughter for a pony ride, she drives down to a joint and gets her "reefer." And being high on marijuana, she is in a condition to break the unspoken agreement of silence that protects the women from outsiders. She can confide in Mr. Palmer that Mrs. Vaughan, six months pregnant, has no husband but the one who was killed at Dieppe, three years before. She can give away Mrs. Kendall's secret of the adopted child and take a catlike claw or two at Mrs. Kendall's prudery, fussiness, self-righteousness. Finally she can involve herself in a screaming catfight with Mrs. Kendall, and in the course of it Mr. Palmer can learn about her too, what makes her pupils so large, what is the source of her furious and demented energy.

In that series of scenes the reversal is completed, the idyllic and wistful picture Mr. Palmer started with has been violently shoved aside and the turmoil of suffering and frustrated humanity it has covered is revealed.

And for an ending—there is no ending, actually, since there is no story but only a revelation, what Joyce called an "epiphany"—I had no choice but to drop the original picture back into place. Being cyclic, the story must return upon itself. I closed out the catfight with the coming of the mailman, and the resubmission of all the women to the monotony of their lives. That ending recommended itself not merely as a way of getting out of the rather melodramatic scene of the women fighting, but also as a structural symbol. If the structure and intention of the story are legitimate, this ending ought to have the power of closing the circle, returning us to where we began but with the added understanding and insight that a round trip behind the scenes has provided.

THE CRITICS

Introduction:
Dimensions of His Story Artistry

Although Stegner wrote a great deal about the theory and practice of the short story, not many critics have chosen to write about his short stories. There are, however, many reviews of his three collections, a substantial number in particular in response to the publication of his *Collected Stories* in 1990. This lack of critical review at the time his stories were originally published bears out Stegner's contention that a writer cannot gain a substantial reputation nowadays on the basis of the short story alone—by the time of the publication of his *Collected Stories*, he had already won the Pulitzer Prize and National Book Award for his novels.

I have chosen from these, however, five short essays: one deals with many of the stories, comparing them to Hemingway's short fictions; another examines several stories in respect to Stegner's well-known environmental advocacy; and a third deals with a pair of travel stories. To balance these I have also included two essays that treat in depth individual stories in illuminating ways, "Maiden in a Tower" and "The Blue-Winged Teal."

In his essay "Stegner and Hemingway as Short Story Writers: Some Parallels and Contrasts in Two Masters," Joseph M. Flora compares two writers who offhand would seem to have had little in common. However, Flora points out that a favored focus of both writers was the father-son relationship, and that young Bruce Mason, Stegner's protagonist in his stories of childhood and growing up, has much in common with Hemingway's Nick Adams; he sees similarities between the parents of the two boys as well. In addition to comparing characters and their relationships in the works of the two writers, Flora goes on to discuss similar techniques and similar organizational strategies used in their respective story collections and in doing so provides new insights into Wallace Stegner's methods.

Nancy Owen Nelson also breaks new ground with her original essay "The 'Geography of Hope' in a Depraved Eden: Wallace Stegner's *Col-*

lected Stories." Although Stegner was as well-known for his environmental work as for his writing, hardly any critic has, up to now, taken the trouble to show how Stegner's concern for the environment, particularly his advocacy for wilderness, has been reflected in his short fiction. Professor Nelson examines several stories that illustrate the theme of "a depraved Eden." More specifically, she brings her attention to three related variations of the theme in Stegner's work: the initiation of the innocent into humanity's perverted efforts to order nature; the effects of the absence of primal nature in a "civilized" context; and the validation of untouched nature.

In "Cities of the Living: Disease and the Traveler in *Collected Stories of Wallace Stegner*," Anne Ricketson Zahlan states that "throughout Stegner's short fiction, characters travel into or away from exile, retrace steps to rediscover the past, or explore new paths in quest of new selves." But her focus will be those middle-aged Americans in two stories, "Something Spurious from the Mindanao Deep" and "The City of the Living," who are confronted with "an otherness of land and people that disturbs their image of themselves and destroys their illusions of safety." In examining these stories, Zahlan pays particular attention to the nuances of Stegner's language.

Another aspect of Stegner's short fiction is brought out in James Ellis's "Wallace Stegner's Art of Literary Allusion: *The Marriage of Heaven and Hell* and *Faust* in 'Maiden in a Tower.' " Stegner was unusually well-educated and better read than most writers of fiction, so that it is not surprising to find him using literary allusion, never heavy-handedly, but nevertheless with implications that spread throughout a story, as Ellis demonstrates in his discussion of "Maiden in a Tower." In the final essay, J. M. Ferguson Jr.'s "Cellars of Consciousness: Stegner's 'The Blue-Winged Teal,' " we have once again, as in the Zahlan piece, a close reading of a story, one that Ferguson labels as an initiation story, "perhaps [American literature's] most prominent theme." Here we encounter one of Stegner's favorite themes, identity, as the story's young protagonist searches for his own and his father's and painfully discovers both.

The cumulative impression of these essays is how varied and rich Wallace Stegner's stories are, how well he mastered the techniques of characterization and description, and how skillfully he employed the tools of the implicit—image, metaphor, and irony.

Joseph M. Flora

In 1990 Random House published *Collected Stories of Wallace Stegner.* It was a fitting way to celebrate Stegner's eightieth birthday, underscoring Stegner's place in American letters and his contribution to the short story.

The publication of *Collected Stories* invites us to consider the contours of Stegner's work in the short story, work that is likely complete. As Stegner observes in the book's Foreword, he has not written a short story for many years.[1]

Considering his work in the genre complete, then, I propose looking at *Collected Stories* to see what the arrangement of the stories might say about the shape of Stegner's two earlier short story collections: *The Women on the Wall* (1950) and *The City of the Living and 7 Other Stories* (1956). Through this exploration, I wish to probe the place of the short story in Stegner's career and to suggest some important influences on those stories.

Two years before the Stegner collection, *The Complete Short Stories of Ernest Hemingway* (not quite complete) had reminded us of Hemingway's devotion to the form, even the centrality of the genre to his career. Although the genre is not central to Stegner, the pairing seems to me nevertheless useful. For Stegner did share some striking affinities with Hemingway, and Stegner's first short story collection in accumulative force bears striking likenesses to Hemingway's first major collection, *In Our Time* (1925).

For me, and probably for other readers, particular Stegner stories often evoke memories of Hemingway stories. To take an obvious instance, "The City of the Living," the final story of Stegner's *Collected Stories* (but second in the collection that is named for it), shares a good deal with Hemingway's "A Day's Wait." Both stories depend on an international contrast; in both an American father keeps vigil over a son with fever. In Hemingway's story, the boy thinks he will die. In Stegner's, the

---

"Stegner and Hemingway as Short Story Writers: Some Parallels and Contrasts in Two Masters," reprinted with permission from *South Dakota Review* 30, no. 1 (September 1992).

father believes that the typhoid fever will take his son. There is learning for both fathers, and probably for both sons—though Stegner is not as concerned with the son's personality as with the father's. Waiting is the significant action of both stories. With Stegner, as with Hemingway, the short story often emphasized quiet moments, internal rather than external action.

Comparison between Stegner's short stories and Hemingway's is almost inevitable because Stegner is like Hemingway in making father-son relationships a favored focus. "A Day's Wait" and "The City of the Dead" are among the instances of stories from the father's perspective. In Hemingway's *In Our Time* and in Stegner's *The Women on the Wall* the reader approaches father-son pairings from the son's perspective. Indeed, both writers continued to favor this angle of vision for some time, as later collections of both authors reveal. Both writers had to probe in fictional guise their own relationships with their fathers before they could treat their relationship with their own sons.[2]

Early in his career, Hemingway had attempted a Nick novel, but "Along with Youth" did not progress vary far. Once he placed Nick in a short story, Hemingway found he could turn to him easily. Nick Adams, though not the protagonist of every story in *In Our Time*, is certainly the chief character of that book. There, in the context of a collection of linked stories, he takes on much of the force of a character from a novel. In fact, a recent reading of *In Our Time* suggests that every story is a Nick story; when Nick is not a character, he is author.[3] Because Nick was a persona as much as character, Hemingway would continue to make Nick an important character in his stories. Nick appeared in several stories of *Men Without Women* (1927) and *Winner Take Nothing* (1933) as well. At Hemingway's death a novel about Nick was among his unfinished works (readers of *The Complete Short Stories of Ernest Hemingway* know it as "The Last Good Country").

The young Bruce Mason (firm establishment of the last name awaited his reincarnation in a novel) is a recurring character in several stories of *The Women on the Wall;* in "The Chink" the unnamed narrator is almost certainly Bruce. Bruce also appears as a character in stories that went into Stegner's second story collection, *The City of the Living,* though his identity was not clear until Bruce's disguises were removed and those stories became part of Stegner's novel *Recapitulation* (1979). The Bruce stories collected in *The Women on the Wall* (excepting "In the Twilight" and "The Chink") had made their way into Stegner's novel *The Big Rock Candy Mountain* (1943). Seven years later, their publication in

The Women on the Wall reasserted their identity as short stories. Although Hemingway's Nick seemed to resist the novel form, Stegner's Bruce made his way into stories less minimalist in technique than Hemingway's usually are (to be sure Hemingway's stories of the 1930s tended to expand) and the chronicle of Bruce and his family provided the basis for the novel that most critics consider Stegner's first major work. From the start, Bruce belonged with such apprenticeship heroes as Wolfe's Eugene Gant as well as with Nick.[4]

Primarily, however, it is Bruce in his more youthful stages that puts us in mind of Nick Adams—especially as Stegner defines him as the son of Bo and Elsa Mason. Bruce's mother (not called by name in the stories) is long suffering and loving. Were her husband more in tune with her longings, she might have counted herself happy in the rigors of the demands of her life on the Saskatchewan frontier. As it is, however, a great gulf between them is often evident. Stegner emphasizes their differences in "Butcher Bird," which is "The Doctor and the Doctor's Wife" of *The Women on the Wall*. A gun is a prominent symbol in both stories, the difference being that Bruce's mother not only sees its symbolic importance, but she is able to articulate something important about her husband: " 'The minute you get a gun in your hand you start feeling better,' she said. 'It's just a shame you weren't born fifty years sooner' " (p. 156). Too much of the frontier is gone for the likes of a Bo Mason, and for Dr. Adams, too—though Mrs. Adams is too self-engrossed to see that reality. Whatever redeemable features Mrs. Adams may have had, Hemingway kept them fairly hidden from view. In only one other story would he ever let her speak and act—he had cast her character in steel in "The Doctor and the Doctor's Wife." About the doctor's weaknesses, Hemingway was more understanding, and Hemingway portrays him in five stories.[5]

Stegner painted Bruce's parents on a broad canvas, and he could return to both of them, with equal ease. Bo is the more complex character of the parents, freer than Dr. Adams to give vent to the dark side of his character. Stegner portrays that dark side in "Goin' to Town," a story set on a Fourth of July. (It may be profitably set next to Hemingway's Fourth of July story, "Ten Indians.") Even while portraying the Masons in the short story form, Stegner realized that he needed numerous angles and situations to delineate Bruce's heritage. Often, of course, Bruce is like Nick—stunned by the complexities of adult life around him, trying to make sense of an existence where cruelty and death are always lying in wait. Stegner's stories about Bruce reveal a Stegner presenting both parents as round characters (revealing strengths and weaknesses of both). Hemingway's reluctance to approach the Adamses in this way helps explain why Nick resisted so long and so successfully Hemingway's efforts to get him into a novel.

Stegner's approach to his fiction is, furthermore, like Hemingway's in its dominant biographical impulse—an impulse Stegner frankly acknowledges. In the Foreword to *Collected Stories* Stegner is direct and honest about the role of biography. Hemingway could tease a reader about such matters—as he certainly did in "The Art of the Short Story," written in his late years as a preface to a proposed collection of his short stories. In his Foreword, Stegner acknowledges that the thirty-one stories of the collection "do make a sort of personal record." He says, "I lived them, either as participant or spectator or auditor, before I made fictions of them" (p. ix). Although Hemingway did not view any Caesarean birth in an Indian Camp, his stories are usually set in terrain he knew well, and "Indian Camp" is no exception. Hemingway's stories often give fictional guise to events and persons he knew—certainly such was the case when he portrayed Nick Adams. He would not question much Stegner's declaration about his method: "If art is a by-product of living, and I believe it is, then I want my own efforts to stay as close to earth and human experience as possible—and the only earth I know is the one I have lived on, the only human experience I am at all sure of is my own" (p. ix). In recent years, some critics have been working to make Hemingway's later efforts more post-modern than modern. Particularly as they discuss unfinished fictions or discarded fragments from completed work, they urge this thesis—often unconvincingly. Hemingway's impulse like Stegner's was to prefer a realistic mode—"to stay as close to earth and human experience as possible" (p. ix). Hemingway might combine surface reality with literary allusions (Gertrude Stein charged that his work had the odor of the museum), but the realistic and autobiographical base remained pronounced in most of his writing.

To be sure, Hemingway was attracted to and participated in modernistic techniques that challenged older narrative conventions. *In Our Time* marked him as one of the participants in the school that wanted to make new things. His first collection treated autobiographical experience with devices of concealment as well as straight narration. Although Nick is the chief character of this work, Hemingway arranged his stories about Nick to create a strong sense of disjunctiveness. Nick is not always a character in the stories, and brief interchapters keep interrupting the progression of more conventional stories. While Hemingway follows Nick's growing up to the realities of his time, he jars us to contemplation of those realities through regular interruptions of Nick's progress. Even the two parts of "Big Two-Hearted River" are separated by "Chapter XV," the vignette about the death of Sam Cardinella.

When Stegner came to arrange the stories of *The Women on the Wall,* he chose to interrupt the straight chronological account of Bruce's life, highlighting thereby the suggestiveness of the Bruce stories. The most notable instance of such disjunctiveness is in the handling of "Goin' to Town" and "Two Rivers." These stories treat events in Bruce's life on successive days. In a novelistic progression, one would follow after the other—as happens in *The Big Rock Candy Mountain.* In *The Women on the Wall,* Stegner separates these two stories, interjecting both "The View from the Balcony" and "The Volcano" between them. The separation enables the reader to begin emotionally fresh, to view Bruce and his parents with greater objectivity—identification having been checked. The closest parallel to these stories in *In Our Time* would be "The End of Something" and "The Three-Day Blow," stories separated by a matter of weeks but both related to Nick's experience of breaking up with Marge. While placing the stories next to each other, Hemingway has an interchapter between them. Stegner breaks the narrative of Bruce's life even more emphatically, for the stories he places between the Bruce stories take place some fifteen or so years after the events of those "companion" Bruce stories.

Of the eighteen stories that became *The Women on the Wall,* eight are Bruce stories. He is unnamed in four of these stories, though he is recognizable. Stegner earlier incorporated six of the eight stories into *The Big Rock Candy Mountain.* "In the Twilight" and "The Chink" exist only as short stories, the latter being the only first-person story of the collection. Twice Bruce stories follow each other. "In the Twilight" and "Butcher Bird" provide the first instance. But the focus is very different, for Bruce is protagonist in "In the Twilight"; his parents provide the focus of "Butcher Bird." With the progression of "The Colt," "The Chink," and "Chip Off the Old Block," the effect is once again disjunctiveness—precisely because "The Chink" is a first person narrative and because Bruce's name is not used.[6] We see him only briefly in "Chip Off the Old Block," where the portrait is of his brother Chet. In other words, one continues to have the sense of reading stories that are related, but not units of a novel.

When he arranged the sequence of *The Women on the Wall,* Stegner seems quite consciously to have enhanced that sense of the disjunctive.

In his Foreword to *Collected Stories* he explains that he did not "attempt to arrange these stories so that they make a progression from simplicity to complexity, past to present, primitive to civilized, sensuous to intellectual" (p. x). Because in the Bruce stories of *The Women on the Wall* the progression is basically chronological, there is some movement towards greater civilization, greater intellectual content, for although Bruce is preadolescent in all those stories, he is sensitive and ready for moral and intellectual growth—and many of the stories that follow *The Women on the Wall* stories, especially those that were part of *The City of the Living*, do have perspectives of increased sophistication and intellectual maturity. Nevertheless, Stegner reports that the stories "lie as they fell, perhaps because I don't believe there is any clear progression to illustrate, or that this journey has any clear destination" (p. x). Perhaps.

We need to keep in mind, however, that although Stegner did not "update" his stories, he did reflect on the order of their original arrangement—an arrangement that served to interrupt easy progression toward maturity. Indeed, Stegner had made important choices when he shaped *The Women on the Wall* and *The City of the Living*. The decisions for the arrangement of the first collection are the more interesting, in part because they involved including stories that had made their way into a novel and excluding a number of previously published stories. Stegner has maintained the validity of those decisions; no story excluded from *The Women on the Wall* later made its way into *Collected Stories*. (When Hemingway had earned the right to his comparable collection, he was able to add "Up in Michigan," placing it close to the place in *In Our Time* where it would logically have gone, thereby correcting the censorship imposed by earlier publishing codes.) And Stegner had not arranged the stories for *The Women on the Wall* in the order of composition or publication. Just as Hemingway maintained to Dos Passos that there was a satisfying sense of unity to *In Our Time*, Stegner seems to have found something like that unity for *The Women on the Wall*. He made one change in ordering those stories for *Collected Stories*. He moved the Bruce story "Buglesong" from fourth position to first—an effective change for the disjunctive mode that follows. It places Bruce's innocence in the reader's consciousness early, before the four stories of adult focus that follow. In only one of those stories do we see children. Because children and the relationship between parent and child are important in stories that follow as well as in many of those of *The City of the Living*, Stegner appropriately strikes the chord early in *Collected Stories* through his shifting of "Buglesong."

One other reordering effectively enhances that emphasis in *Collected Stories*. Stegner moved "The Traveler" from final position in *The City of the Living* sequence to opening position of the entire collection, signaling thereby that the ordering of *The City of the Living* was less crucial than the ordering for *The Women on the Wall*. Had Stegner not moved the story, it would have been the twenty-sixth story in *Collected Stories*. By moving it to first position, Stegner highlights the journey metaphor that overarches so many of the stories. Although pilgrimage is a common metaphor for human life, Stegner gives the metaphor his own signature. "The Traveler" strikes the proper note for *Collected Stories* as well as the stories of *The Women on the Wall*, which it now introduces, becoming an allegorical invitation or prelude.

The unnamed protagonist in "The Traveler" is a middle-aged salesman marooned in severe winter weather on a White Christmas night when his car fails him in isolated country. Because his product is pharmaceutical drugs, survival is doubly the issue. The salesman is unnamed (so is the locale) because he becomes all of us. An American sturdily nurtured on doctrines of self-reliance, he must conclude: "A man was dependent on too many people; he was at everybody's mercy" (p. 6). Eventually, he makes his way to a farm house where he finds a young boy who is also confronting an emergency. An orphan, the boy needs to get help for his grandfather, who has had a stroke or heart attack, and the narrator becomes involved in that rescue effort. The point of Stegner's story is not the outcome of this particular drama, but its relevance in a very broad sense. The boy prefigures dilemmas of Bruce Mason and Andy Mount ("The Hostage" and *Second Growth*). Sensitive and capable, both will have to overcome powerful odds in order to realize their potential (Bruce has greater success than Andy in those attempts). In "The Traveler" the salesman, probably not in the occupation he might have aspired to as a youth, is intelligent and sensitive, exemplifying the adult mentality Stegner's protagonists usually have. Not only survival, but meaningful identity engross Stegner—as this lead story of *Collected Stories* reveals. Looking at the boy, the salesman in an epiphanal moment recognizes himself. Stegner, like Hemingway, strives in his short stories for the suggestive. The final paragraph of "The Traveler" prepares us for numerous epiphanies of *Collected Stories:*

> Along the road he had never driven he went swiftly towards an unknown farm and an unknown town, to distribute according to some wise law part of the burden of the boy's emergency and his own; but he

bore in his mind, bright as moonlight over snow, a vivid wonder, almost an awe. For from the most chronic and incurable of ills, identity, he had looked outward and for one unmistakable instant recognized himself. (p. 11)

First rather than last was the right place for Stegner to place this story.

Thereafter, with the single alteration I have identified, the reader of *Collected Stories* finds stories in the order of *The Women on the Wall.* That collection, as I have suggested, explores most of the basic concerns of *In Our Time*—innocence, loss of innocence, survival, bravery and cowardice, travel, memory. As I have argued, Stegner uses disjunctiveness of placement to affect the way we experience those themes. I do not insist that he had Hemingway's book consciously in mind (though as a teacher and student of the short story, Stegner had certainly paid attention to Hemingway's work), but his interest in rendering his own experience quite naturally made his collection another depiction of life "in our time."

Because Stegner was a decade younger than Hemingway, the time frame is not quite the same. Stegner was too young to join Hemingway, Cummings, Dos Passos in any ambulance units to World War I. But war— from somewhat different perspectives—is surely one of the important subjects of his first collection of short stories. The title story of *The Women on the Wall* does more than identify one of the strongest stories; it identifies the importance of the war theme to the collection. Quite insistently, the stories keep coming back to the impact war has on human lives. For almost all of the stories written in the 1940s, the war under scrutiny, not surprisingly, is World War II. "The Berry Patch," "The Women on the Wall," and "The Volcano" are set during the actual years of the war. "The View from the Balcony" portrays the lives of graduate students who have just returned from that war, the narrative voice being that of an Englishwoman who had survived Hitler's bombs. The Bruce stories, on the other hand, evoke the horrors of World War I. In "Butcher Bird" Mr. Garfield, a transplanted Englishman, is so conscious of the trench warfare then in progress that he no longer wishes to keep his gun. When he gives it to Bruce, he asks that Bruce not use the gun on nonpredatory animals. Bruce's father, not imaginatively involved with the Great War, has nothing but contempt for Mr. Garfield, and shoots a sparrow with Bruce's gun to protest what he sees as Garfield's effeminacy. Thus, *The Women on the Wall* interweaves stories that reveal aspects of both world wars.

Stegner's stories provide, additionally, a vivid portrayal of an accompaniment of World War I that reached dramatically into many American lives—the influenza epidemic of 1918. "The Chink" portrays the effects of provincial thinking and failure to defend "the other" from racial bigotry. In this Bruce story, Bruce and his schoolmates lock a Chinese laborer in a privy that they have overturned as a part of their Halloween pranks. Their pranks scarcely begun, the pranksters are soon put to more noble tasks, as the school principal brings news of the flu epidemic. Bruce helps spread the word, but like the others does nothing to rescue Mah Li from his prison. Soon severely ill with the flu, Bruce awakens days later to find that Mah Li spent the night in that prison and has died from influenza. Bruce must live then with the guilt of his own action and inaction. "Chip Off the Old Block" portrays the bravery of Bruce's brother Chet after Bruce and his parents are carried to the infirmary as victims of the influenza. When they return home on November 11, a memorable celebration of the end of the war is in progress. In several ways, then, war asserts its presence in *The Women on the Wall*, at least as insistently as it does in *In Our Time*.

Not a combatant, Stegner portrayed the effects of war on the home front. In "The Berry Patch" we listen as a young soldier and his wife talk and define the shape that war has given their lives as a couple. Stegner's quiet story is in the mode of a dramatic dialogue by Robert Frost. Especially from the perspective of the 1990s, we note Stegner's focus on the woman and her insistence on the new independence that her responsibilities of running the farm have brought into her life. In "The Women on the Wall," Stegner's central consciousness is that of an older writer-historian, a bachelor who has viewed some of life's realities from a safe distance. As the story begins, he sentimentalizes the lives of the Penelopes who gather at the wall along the ocean to wait for the postman, hoping he brings news from their husbands fighting on Pacific fronts. Brought into direct contact with the women, the narrator comes to view their waiting more realistically.

In "The Volcano," perhaps the most Hemingwayesque story of the collection, an unnamed American, most likely a reporter, is in Mexico to see first hand the devastation from the erupting volcano Paricutín:

> The village of Paricutín, on the other side, had been buried completely under the lava that was death both definite and sudden. But this slow death that fell like the light rain, this gradual something that drooped the pines and covered the holes of the little animals and mounded the roofs and choked the trees, this dying village through which ghosts went in silence, was something else. It was a thing Mexicans had

always known, in one form or another, else there would not be in so many of their paintings the figure of the robed skeleton, the walking Death. They were patient under it, they accepted it—but the American did not like to remember how alive the eyes of the Indian girls had been as they waded through the ashes with their little sisters on their backs. (p. 111)

The volcano, Stegner means us to see, is much like the global war then in progress. As in "The Berry Patch," the war theme gradually surfaces as major. When that emphasis is clear, the dialogue appears markedly in the Hemingway manner:

"I have conceived a great hatred for this thing," the American said finally. "It is a thing I have always known and always hated. It is something which kills."

"Truly," the driver said. "I have felt it, as those who are in the war must feel the war."

"Yes," the American said.

"You have friends in the war?"

"Sons," the American said. "One is now a prisoner in Germany."

"*Ai,*" the driver said, with sympathy. He hesitated a minute, as if hunting for the correct thing to say to one whose sons were captives of the enemy. "You hear from him?" he said. "How does he endure his captivity?"

"How does one endure anything?" the American said. "I suppose he hates it and endures it, that is all." He looked out the window, raised his shoulders. "I have heard once only," he said for politeness sake. (p. 117)[7]

In many stories of *The Women in the Wall* Stegner keeps his focus on the shocked innocence of a young male protagonist, although that was not his focus in the war stories. (The startled young male was central to many of Hemingway's stories.) But Stegner has created memorable stories about other aspects of war and its aftermath, the sensibilities of women important in several of them. *The Women on the Wall* has considerable power as a study of various faces of war. As such it may appropriately be set next to *In Our Time.*

Although Stegner had learned the lessons of disjunctiveness and the modernistic methods that *In Our Time* demonstrated, he knew also that Hemingway's book had not developed in a vacuum. Hemingway's models were Joyce's *Dubliners* (1914) and Anderson's *Winesburg, Ohio* (1919). By placing "The Sweetness of the Twisted Apples" last in *The Women on the Wall,* Stegner reminded his readers of Anderson's pivotal role in the new freedom Anderson had pioneered for the American short story and the possibilities for books of linked short stories that used distinctiveness as a device, collections that created a unity other than progressive narration. Stegner's title echoes a key line from Anderson's story "Paper Pills" from *Winesburg.* "The Sweetness of the Twisted Apples" portrays a lovable "grotesque" who, like the Alice Hindman of Anderson's "Adventure," has learned that many must live and die alone, be it in Winesburg or the remote Vermont setting of Stegner's story. (Like Anderson, Stegner presented many sympathetic portraits of women in his first collection.)[8] But because of the Bruce stories and the constant reminders of the world wars, *In Our Time* remains the more natural analog to Stegner's first collection.

Although *The Women on the Wall* was Stegner's first collection of stories, it was his *ninth* book, not counting his doctoral dissertation. (Four of those works were novels, two were novelettes.) At the time of its publication, Stegner was an established author, usually ranked among his country's important writers. *In Our Time* came at a very different point in Hemingway's career. When it was published, Hemingway was virtually an unknown writer in America, though his talent was recognized in Paris among the expatriates who played so dominant a role in the development of literary modernism. Hemingway's first books, *Three Stories and Ten Poems* (1923) and *in our time* (1924), had been published by Bill Bird's *Three Mountain Press* in modest printings. It was *In Our Time,* Hemingway's first book to be published by a commercial publisher, that marked him as an important writer, one for whom commercial publishers would compete. His success in shorter fictional units established, Hemingway then resumed the challenge of the novel. Stegner's course is the reverse of Hemingway's, for he was an established writer in the novel before his first short story collection came into being. His first book, *Remembering Laughter* (1937), had won him a major prize in Little, Brown's short novel competition.

This publishing history emphasizes that the short story was more essential to Hemingway than to Stegner. Hemingway envisioned alternating novels and short story collections as a good practice. *Men Without Women* (1927) followed *The Sun Also Rises* (1926). *Winner Take Nothing* (1933) followed *A Farewell to Arms* (1929) and *Death in the Afternoon* (1932). *The Fifth Column and the First Forty-nine Stories* (1938) followed *Green Hills of Africa* (1935) and *To Have and Have Not* (1937). Although no other collections appeared in Hemingway's life, he continued to contemplate such gatherings and to discuss them with Scribner's. His enthusiasm for the short story ebbed and flowed some, but the form remained useful to him throughout his life. He continued to write short stories almost to his death.

Stegner planned no such interweaving between novels and short story collections, the short story being less central to his purposes than to Hemingway's. Although *The Women on the Wall* is like *In Our Time* in many ways, as we have noted, several stories in it made their way into novels. Stegner's second story collection, *The City of the Living and 7 Other Stories*, is more discrete in its parts as its full title suggests. As we have observed, for *Collected Stories* Stegner moved "The Traveler," the last story of *The City*, completely out of this sequence, making it play more as prelude to the whole volume. The proportions of Stegner's second collection also indicate how much closer he had moved in his preference for longer units. "Field Guide to the Western Birds," the true showpiece of Stegner's second collection, is a long short story—really a novella. Eventually, it became part of the novel *All the Little Live Things* (1967). Three other stories in the collection—"The Blue-Winged Teal," "Impasse," and "Maiden in a Tower"—were eventually units in the second Bruce novel, *Recapitulation* (1979). When the *Collected Stories* appeared some thirty-four years following the publication of Stegner's second story collection, there were only five stories to add. Three of them were stories that had been part of *Wolf Willow* (1962), and one of those, "Genesis," was novella-length.

Clearly, the attraction of the short story form was less intense for Stegner than for Hemingway. In his Foreword to *Collected Stories*, Stegner declares the short story "a young writer's form, made for discoveries and nuances and epiphanies and superbly adapted for trial syntheses." He found that the novel "tended to swallow and absorb potential stories" and "found fairly early that even stories begun without the intention of being anything but independent tended to cluster, wanting to be part of something longer" (p. x). For Hemingway, the attraction and possibilities of the short story form continued to allure. How differently he ended his preface to *The First Forty-nine:* "I would like to live long enough to write three more novels and twenty-five more stories. I know some pretty good ones."[9] He didn't write the twenty-five, but he came closer than readers sometimes think—even closer if we consider *A Moveable Feast* as a collection of short fictions. In Stegner's case, we do find the essential novelist. But, as his *Collected Stories* make clear, during the course of his continued career, he crafted some able stories, and *The*

Women on the Wall stories may be read as a collection that is more than a collection, where story comments on story—much as in *In Our Time*.

Notes

1. *Collected Stories of Wallace Stegner* (New York: Random House, 1990), p. x. Future references to this collection will be cited parenthetically in the text.

2. One of the burdens both Hemingway and Stegner shared—and eventually dealt with in their fiction—was the suicide of their own fathers. When Clarence Hemingway shot himself on December 26, 1928, Ernest was twenty-nine years old. When George Stegner shot himself in 1940, Wallace was thirty-one years old.

3. See Debra A. Moddelmog, "The Unifying Consciousness of a Divided Conscience: Nick Adams as Author of *In Our Time*," *American Literature*, 60 (December 1988): 591–610. Moddelmog's essay is reprinted in *New Critical Approaches to the Short Stories of Ernest Hemingway*, ed. Jackson J. Benson (Durham: Duke University Press, 1990), pp. 18–32.

4. Unlike Nick, Bruce did not (apparently) become a writer, but made his mark as an ambassador. Yet Bruce has the temperament of a writer. When he was a college student, he belonged to the artistic crowd; he trained in the humanities. The single first-person Bruce story ("The Chink") lets us know how strong the creative and the confessional are in his make-up. Other ambassadors have written fiction, why not Bruce? If we consider the discursive structures of *The Women on the Wall*, we might also be tempted to see every story of the book as a Bruce story. I doubt, however, that such was consciously part of Stegner's purpose—just as I doubt that when Hemingway wrote "My Old Man" he considered it a Nick story. Nevertheless, Moddelmog's analysis of the unifying consciousness in *In Our Time* (see footnote 3) is immensely useful. So is attention to the unifying consciousness of *The Women on the Wall*. The parallels between that work and *In Our Time* become even more numerous and striking when we note the unifying consciousness in each.

5. When we see Mrs. Adams in "Now I Lay Me," it is through Nick's memory, and she speaks only a single telling line: "I've been cleaning out the basement, dear." In addition to "The Doctor and the Doctor's Wife," we see the doctor in "Indian Camp" and "Ten Indians"—and, again through Nick's memory, in "Now I Lay Me" and "Fathers and Sons."

In Stegner's *Recapitulation* (Garden City: Doubleday, 1979) a mature Bruce Mason might be expressing a realization of Nick Adams in his middle age: "He told himself that it is easy enough to recover from a girl, who represents to some extent a choice. It is not so easy to recover from parents, who are fate" (264).

6. Hemingway wrote several first person Nick stories, but he did not always use Nick's name in them. The most famous instance is "The Light of

the World," which most critics have long considered a Nick story narrated by Nick.

7. Before World War II ended, Hemingway found himself in a position similar to that of the American of Stegner's story. John (Bumby) Hemingway was a prisoner of the Germans, though "Volcano" slightly precedes his capture. The story first appeared in *Harpers* in September 1944; John was reported missing in action on October 7, 1944, later as captured.

8. Although Stegner is paying tribute to Anderson, he achieves much more in the story. We may glean a good deal about its discursive content and its place in *The Women on the Wall* by placing it next to "Big Two-Hearted River"— the masterful story that came last in *In Our Time*. Troubled relationships between a man and a women are as prominent in Stegner's collection as in Hemingway's—the marriages of Bruce's and Nick's parents being merely the most obvious examples. "Beyond the Glass Mountain," the first story in *The Women on the Wall*, shows us a marriage in which the woman seems bent on destroying her husband; its narrative voice is that of a male who has protected himself by not marrying. In "The Sweetness of the Twisted Apples" we journey into the wilderness (not as remote as the country of the "Big Two-Hearted River," to be sure) with an artist and his wife. This artist has not taken his journey alone and does not seem compelled to leave behind "various needs." What is important is that he is fulfilling the need to create—and in the company of his wife, a woman alert and sensitive.

9. *The Fifth Column and the First Forty-nine Stories* (New York: Charles Scribner's Sons, 1938), p. vii.

Nancy Owen Nelson

In Wallace Stegner's short story "The Sweetness of the Twisted Apples," published in his 1990 *Collected Stories*, he offers a compelling metaphor for the despoiled Eden that is inherent in much of his writing:

> Against the crawling edge of woods and the eyeless emptiness of the farmhouse, against the whole irrational patternlessness of decay, the orchard kept its design. Though the tops were unpruned and overgrown, the trunks marched where a farmer's hands had set them to march, and among the thinning leaves hung an unbelievably heavy crop of runty apples, reddening for no harvest.[1]

This description points clearly to Stegner's alignment with the *preservationist* rather than the *conservationist* position, his evolving concern that, as Americans, we have been led to exploit the free land of our heritage in an effort to fulfill our notions of the American Dream.[2] The farmer in the story, representative of mankind's effort to civilize and control (conserve) nature, has created an order in the orchard that, now left to decay, serves as a backdrop for the lost hope of an ungainly Vermont woman who visits it.

This theme of a depraved Eden, so clearly delineated in as late a work as *Crossing to Safety* (1987), is a strong thread running through the *Collected Stories*. A paradox lies in the notion that while the "serpent" is present in and, in fact, "valid[ates]" the garden even in its most primal and perfect form,[3] man engulfed in "civilization" and its effects is more severely threatened by depravity. As I see it, the stories illustrate three versions of this paradoxical theme: the innocent characters' initiation into man's perverted efforts to order nature; the effects of the absence of primal nature in a "civilized" context; and the validation of untouched nature, which, while it may threaten and tax man's survival,

---

This essay was written specifically for this volume and is published here for the first time by permission of the author.

131

provides him with a "naturalness . . . in nature,"[4] a more desirable state of being, while justly maintaining its inherent purity.

The companion stories "Goin' to Town" and "The Two Rivers" establish the thematic relationships between man, nature, and civilization in Stegner's work. The young protagonist Brucie is disappointed in the first story by the breakdown of the family's Ford on July 4, when they had plans to attend the day's festivities at Chinook, a town near the "Mountains of the Moon" (*Collected Stories*, 76). "Goin' to Town" is a story of hopelessness; the boy watches the day slip by while his father tries to start the car. Early in the story, Brucie sees himself as larger than nature, his artificial power (provided by the technology of the car and the potential visit to town) rendering him "verti[cal] in all that spread of horizontal land[;] he sensed how the prairie shrank on this morning and how he himself grew" (75). In a short time, however, the boy is reduced to a state of "dull hopelessness. . . . Shoulders sagging, tears trembling to fall, his jaw aching with the need to cry." (83). Remembering bitterly his lost sense of power, he ends the story by making a six-foot round circle of his own "delicately exact footprints" in the mud, a meager and hopeless effort to *order* nature (84).

The second and companion story, "Two Rivers," which takes place the next day, resolves Brucie's problem by allowing him to explore, on a family picnic to the "Mountains on the Moon," nature in its primal form in both his present and his memory. In contrast to the hopelessness of "Goin' to Town," this story focuses on the primal beauty of the mountains and Brucie's response to it. Enroute to the mountains, Brucie recalls a mountain memory—a stream, and "mashed ripe blackberries in his hand" (119). This dip into his primal mind is interrupted by the discovery of a huge snake engorging a gopher. Here Stegner reminds us of the necessary presence of the snake in the otherwise untouched Garden; its juxtaposition with Brucie's memory of a past experience in the mountains reinforces the primal symbol of Eden. The story ends hopefully as Brucie sees the "very real" mountains in their true primal power: he sees "the steep thrust of the mountains, purpling in the shadows, the rock glowing golden-red far back on the faces of the inner peaks" (126). Here the power remains within primal nature, not in the artificial mechanism of man.

Other initiation stories, "In the Twilight," "Butcher Bird," and "The Colt," involve a young boy's realistic encounter with man's cruel quest for power over the creatures of nature. Sickened by his daily task of bringing slop to the pig, Bruce, the protagonist in "In the Twilight," learns a hard lesson about the realities of slaughtering. Thinking he is ready to observe the killing of the pig, feeling "excited" by the prospect of the kill (140), Bruce instead finds the killing "intolerable . . . a death that did not want to die, a vast, greedy life hurt and dying and shrilling its pain" (141). Observing that the carcass of the pig looks "innocent and harmless" hanging from a rope, the boy is confronted by his father blowing air into the pig's bladder; he "[sees] the bladder swell and tighten and grow round, big as a soccer ball" (146). Bruce finally overcomes his weakness by participating in the cruelty, "that ritual act of kicking the sow's insides around, dirtying them in the dust of the field, taking out on them his own shame and his own fear and hatred and disbelief" (146). Fully initiated into a role as "controller" of nature, Bruce feels "triumphant" and "full of life" (146).

Likewise, in "Butcher Bird" the boy protagonist witnesses an even more deliberate cruelty as his father, jealous of neighbor Garfield's finer sensibilities, takes a gun that Garfield has given the boy and coldly shoots an innocent sparrow. The father, in his deliberate act of cruelty, emulates the more natural process of a pesky butcher bird, which preys upon innocent creatures such as sparrows.

In yet another initiation story, "The Colt," young Bruce becomes attached to Socks, a colt whose front legs have been broken. Bruce's efforts to heal the colt fail, and his father, following the credo to destroy that which is flawed in nature, has Bruce sell the colt to another man who is supposed to keep the animal until spring. But Bruce is faced with the harsh reality of man's abuse of nature when the family passes by the "bloated skinned body of the colt, the chestnut hair left a little way above the hooves, the iron braces still on the broken front legs" (190). The degradation of nature is the more complete with the skinning of Bruce's beloved pet.

Two stories that deal with the second theme—the adult perspective on the depraved Eden—are "Carrion Spring" and "The Sweetness of the Twisted Apples." In the former story, a young couple, Molly and Ray, wrestle with whether to stay in the rotten, "hopeless country a hundred miles from nowhere" where they have struggled to make a living (475). Pervaded by a stench from "two acres of carcasses" that had been skinned, the territory near Whitemud, Saskatchewan, has become, for Molly, a dismal country. But for Ray the land holds hope—an investment in a cattle ranch. The serpent in their relationship, the disagreement over whether to stay, is interrupted by Molly's discovery of an orphaned puppy, a renewal of hope for her. Finding the natural beauty overwhelms the depravity of the stench; Molly smells a crocus, "only a mild freshness . . . maybe enough to cover the scent of carrion" (485). In her final words Molly concedes to Ray's efforts to try to succeed in a depraved Eden.

"The Sweetness of the Twisted Apples," earlier mentioned, involves Margaret and her artist husband Ross's discovery of an old, deserted apple orchard in Vermont. Here, where man once lived, the vestiges of civilization involve such images as a "barely-traveled road" (221), "a stone wall . . . swallowed in impenetrable brush," and a "dead-windowed house" (222). The only farm folk remaining are a woman and her "wizened, dark-featured" (223) daughter, whose possibilities have been tragically limited by the desertion of a young man who often courted her at the apple orchard. In this story Stegner draws a clear picture of the depravity of Eden in what is left from man's efforts toward order. Near the orchard Margaret sits in a deserted graveyard with " pretentious monuments" dating back to 1778 (225). She reflects on an old grandmother "watching the hill farms go dead like lights going out, watching the decay spread" (225). She finds the road "blighted," with houses and buildings reflecting "failure and death . . . like contagion warnings" (227). Margaret becomes Eve when she tastes the sweet tang of the apples, offering one to her husband. Against this backdrop, the girl, whom Margaret sees as "herself a part of the general decay" (227), tells the story of a young man's courting, then her "disappointment" when he married someone else (228). Like the bittersweet taste of the apples, the girl's tale and man's former efforts to order nature have gone to depravation.

In "Field Guide to the Western Birds" and "He Who Spits at the Sky," two California stories, Stegner illustrates the third theme—man's perversion of nature through civilization. In the first story, Stegner uses Joe Allston, the ironic narrator of *All the Little Live Things*, to view the civilization of lost hope, purity, and innocence. As an "ex-literary agent" (311), Allston identifies himself as an "incipient birdwatcher" (315), who, with his wife Ruth, attends a cocktail party designed to give public exposure to an up-and-coming pianist, Kaminski. The narrator pursues his point of view as birdwatcher throughout the party, reporting the artificiality of California society and the subsequent behavior of the partygoers. Reflected in "artificial moonlight," this food is described in its lush perversion:

A landslide, an avalanche: slabs of breast from barbecued turkeys, gobs of oyster dressing, candied yams dripping like honeycomb. . . . Shishkebab ... pickles, olives, celery frizzled in crushed ice, a smorgasbord of smoked salmon, smoked eel, smoked herring, cheeses. Ovens in the *opulent* [my emphasis] barbecue yield corn fingers, garlic bread. ... Carts burdened with ice-cream confections shaped like apples. ... Also pastries, petits fours, napoleons, eclairs." (328–29)

The lush feast is supplemented with a suckling pig reminiscent of Golding's version in *Lord of the Flies*. Trapped in the artifice of the residence, Allston describes a "radiant-heated magic carpet ... abandoned chairs and empty lawn [with] translucent green-blue pool fumes" (342). He finds himself feeling like he is "marooned on a space ship" (342). The perversion is complete when pianist Kaminski plays his pieces imperfectly, yet gets encouraging applause, and, after too many drinks, insults a proper music teacher.

In closing the story, narrator Joe Allston reflects on how he would love to shoot an irritating though "unidentifiable" bird that bashes itself against the window, "hypnotized by the insane hostility of his double" (258). Likewise, Joe feels contempt for those he observed at the party the evening before. He will "watch the fool thing [the bird] as long as [he] can stand it, and ruminate on the insanities of men and birds, and try to convince [him]self that as a local idiocy, an individual aberration, this behavior is not significant" (358). Unable to explain human nature, Joe Allston has nonetheless clearly shown that the artifice and perversion in California society, the attempt to "mirror" nature, does not cultivate man's best self.

In a similar vein, photographer Charlie Prescott, the narrator of "He Who Spits at the Sky," has the opportunity to observe California society at its perverted "best." Set ironically in the "scented evening air of the city of the angels" (487), the story is a revelation of the effects of civilization on man's value system; consequently the piece is rife with imagery of the Garden. Arriving at a party, Prescott is greeted at the door by a tipsy hostess, Debbie Mazur. Prescott observes that, in her condition, "she must have been propped up like an overburdened fruit tree" (489). During the course of the party he is witness to a disagreement between Pepe and Angelina, whose mating, he imagines, would be "corrupt seedbed and poisoned seed and a hatch of snakes and dragons" (505). Seeing them struggling physically in the shadows, Prescott observes that their "heads darted and feinted like the heads of snakes" (506). Pepe's assault on Angelina, though witnessed by Prescott, is refuted by others at the party, who prefer to deny the truth rather than take the bleeding woman to the hospital. In the final scene Prescott, aware of the futility of pressing charges, destroys the evidence in his roll of film. In doing so he reflects the futility expressed in the story's title, which is taken from a Spanish expression, "You spit at the sky, you get it back in the face" (504). When man attempts to control nature he creates an artificial and ultimately damaging climate, one in which the serpent reigns rather than functioning as a lesser part of a larger picture.

In contrast, when man the preservationist allows nature to remain in its primal state in Stegner's stories, he must struggle to survive, but he can survive with dignity. If, like "civilized" man, he attempts to control nature, he will be destroyed. Two Saskatchewan stories, "The Wolfer" and "Genesis," reveal man's confrontation with untouched nature. The narrator of "The Wolfer," a mountie, is on a quest to follow the path of a wolfer, Schultz, who makes the mistake of trying to control the wilds of nature. Schultz is described as a "a savage, a wild man. He hated civilization . . . but it was not civilization that did him in. It was the wild, the very savagery he trusted and thought he controlled" (454). Schultz's hatred of the wolf leads him into a chase during which he ends up shooting his loyal dog. Perplexed, the mountie narrator realizes that Schultz's wildness is caused by his hatred of the wolves, whom he wants to control. He speculates that Schultz's hound, which he had trained so well to kill, had turned on Schultz himself, causing him to shoot the animal—"his own poison had turned into an enemy" (468).

The narrator, who never finds Schultz, realizes the futility of his own quest when he sees all footprints obliterated by nature—a Chinook, or warm spring wind—leading to "ambiguity" (469). Man's efforts to control raw nature end in oblivion.

In his story "Genesis," a novella about young Englishman Rusty Cullen and his experience on a winter cattle drive in Saskatchewan, Stegner explores, in a powerful and graphic way, man's struggles to survive in primal nature. The story is literally one of death and rebirth, Rusty's initiation into the Garden, and his coming to terms with his manhood and need for camaraderie. In this story nature is characterized as brutal and uncontrollable. The efforts of the characters to survive a blizzard during a cattle drive emphasize the primacy of preservation over conservation (or control) of nature in Stegner's philosophy.

While the story is definitely a coming to manhood of Rusty Cullen, it is also a study of man against the character of primal nature. "Genesis," as the title indicates, relies heavily on Biblical symbolism related to the creation of man and his sin in the Garden. In the early pages, nature is seen through Rusty's eyes as "pre"-Creation, with

> a cleanness like the blade of a knife, a distance without limits, a horizon that did not bound the world but only suggested endless space beyond ... [a] white and yellow world, the bowl of the colorless sky unbearable with light. (380)

Man is definitely finite against infinite nature; to Rusty, the river through the ice "seemed like some dark force from the ancient heart of the earth that could at any time rise around them silently and obliterate their little human noises and tract and restore the plain to its emptiness again" (387).

As the story progresses Stegner uses images of darkness to suggest the destructive end cycle of nature's cycle. As the men struggle through seemingly insurmountable obstacles in the ravaging winter of Saskatchewan, they are confronted with "a chaos of dark and cold and the howl of a wind that sometimes all but lifted them from their feet," a grim reminder of their finitude (402). As Rusty searches for his own salvation, reminders of the serpent in the Garden are the "snake-tongue of the wind" (389), "the wide look [of rope] ... snaking in the air" (390), and time, which "whipped and snaked past in unceasing movement" (430). In its force, nature bears for Rusty a reminder of his own lacking, "a deserved punishment, a predicted retribution, the sort of feeling he used to have in childhood when something tempted him beyond all caution and all warnings" (424).

As a thaw brings the "stink of final decay," the men struggle forward against a "heartless and inhuman [wind], older than earth and totally alien ... savage ... the cannibal spirit" (435). Only when Rusty has struggled not only for himself, but also for Spurlock, who almost dies of exposure, can he begin to experience a rebirth, characterized as the return of feeling to his frozen hands and feet: "Life returned as pain; far down his legs Rusty felt a deep, passionate ache beginning at his feet" (439). Finding love and camaraderie for those he had disdained, his fellow cowboys, Rusty realizes his need for others; as he rests in a warm cabin with the other men, the "ancient implacable wind ... tore away balked and shrill" (450). Here man survives through courage and camaraderie, not through efforts to control nature. Nature, on the other hand, remains, in all of its primal power, intact.

137

Wallace Stegner's theme of man's relationship to the environment has been a compelling concern in much of his writing, including his non-fiction. In the essay "Born a Square" he laments the West's exploitation and abuse of the virgin land.[5] In his Overture to his essay collection *The Sound of Mountain Water,* he glorifies the vision of the rivers and canyons near Yellowstone: "All I knew was that it was pure delight to be where the land lifted in peaks and plunged in canyons, and to sniff air thin, spray-cooled, full of pine and spruce smells, and to be so close-seeming to the improbable indigo sky. I gave my heart to the mountains."[6] In "Coda: A Wilderness Letter," he stresses that our efforts to control our environment have brought us close to destruction; instead, he warns, we must adapt the preservationist view—"One means of sanity is to retain a hold on the natural world, to remain, insofar as we can, good animals."[7] As recently as April of 1990, Stegner published an article in *Smithsonian,* "It All Began with Conservation," in which he traces our "breaking" and "subduing" of the wilderness, which has led to the destruction of our environment.[8] However, one of Stegner's most eloquent statements about the errors of our environmental ways is from *American Places.* Here Stegner warns us:

> We are the unfinished product of a long becoming. In our ignorance and hunger and rapacity, in our dream of a better material life, we laid waste the continent and diminished ourselves before any substantial number of us began to feel, little and late, an affinity with it, a dependence on it, an obligation toward it as the indispensable source of everything we hope for.[9]

Indeed, in the *Collected Stories* we can see Wallace Stegner's enduring concern for nature. We can see his realization that although the Garden is rife with temptations mirroring man's flawed nature, man's salvation lies *not* in the artifices of his "civilized" material world but in the preservation of nature in its purest form. As he tells us in "Coda: Wilderness Letter," nature is our "geography of hope" (153).

Notes

1. Wallace Stegner, *Collected Stories of Wallace Stegner* (New York: Random House, 1990), 225. All references to the short stories are from this volume and are cited in the text as *Collected Stories.*
2. See Russell Burrows, "Wallace Stegner's Version of Pastoral," *Western American Literature* 21, no. 1 (May 1990), 15–25, in which he analyzes the Eden

theme in several of Stegner's novels. Hereafter cited in the text.

3. Wallace Stegner, *Crossing to Safety* (New York: Random House, 1987), 172.

4. Jackson J. Benson, " 'Eastering': Wallace Stegner's Love Affair with Vermont in *Crossing to Safety*," *Western American Literature* 25, no. 1 (May 1990), 31.

5. Wallace Stegner, "Born a Square," in *The Sound of Mountain Water* (Garden City, N.Y.: Doubleday & Company, Inc., 1969).

6. Wallace Stegner, Overture to *The Sound of Mountain Water*, 42.

7. Wallace Stegner, "Coda: A Wilderness Letter," in *The Sound of Mountain Water*, 147. Hereafter cited in the text.

8. Wallace Stegner, "It All Began with Conservation," *Smithsonian* (April 1990): 35.

9. Wallace Stegner and Page Stegner, *American Places* (Moscow: University of Idaho Press, 1983), vii.

Anne Ricketson Zahlan

Characterizing his short fiction as "rest stops" along life's journey, Wallace Stegner claims the *Collected Stories* to mark the itinerary in no significant order—they "lie as they fell" ([ix], x). Nevertheless, the volume opens with "The Traveler" stalled on a snowy road in the American West, and closes in a hotel room with another traveler looking out on the Nile. In both stories men involuntarily break journeys, and in encountering boys confront themselves. The unnamed protagonist of "The Traveler" comes face to face with his younger self; Robert Chapman in "The City of the Living" nearly loses his own son to find the beginnings of wisdom in a glimpse of an Egyptian boy at prayer.

More striking than the shared theme of travel is the medicinal link that connects the first and last of Stegner's *Collected Stories*. The traveler "betrayed" by an aging automobile is a salesman of pharmaceuticals who peddles "drugs, some of them designed to cure anything—wonder drugs, sulfas, streptomycin, Aureomycin, penicillin, pills and anti-toxins and unguents . . ." (4). Confronted suddenly with mortality and a boy's need, the "Salesman of wonder cures . . . must now produce something to calm this over-worried boy, restore a dying man" (8). In "The City of the Living," medicines also function paradoxically and even more significantly: playing their therapeutic role in the recovery of the protagonist's dangerously ill son, they serve as ironic image of a dependence on science that, attempting to negate death, appears also to negate life.

Throughout Stegner's short fiction, characters travel into or away from exile, retrace steps to rediscover the past, or explore new paths in quest of new selves. His American homeland can reject immigrants like Mah Li and Mah Jim in "The Chink" or the young Angelinos of "He Who Spits at the Sky," but it can also nurture and teach travelers like Lucy Graham or the young Englishman of "Genesis." Besides the natives and the "foreigners" who range his continent, Stegner also

---

"Cities of the Living: Disease and the Traveler in the *Collected Stories* of Wallace Stegner," reprinted with permission from *Studies in Short Fiction* 29 (1992): 509–15. Copyright © 1992 by Newberry College.

writes about Americans who travel to other parts of "the whole confused world" ([ix]). Despite his apparent comfort with the notion of life as a journey (see [ix]-xi), Stegner's stories of Third-World travel betray an ambivalent response to newly encountered threats to security and well-being. In "The Volcano," North American tourists take sightseeing trips to the site of a Mexican volcano, whose inexorable death-dealing strikes the central observer as parallel to the war raging in Europe. "Something Spurious from the Mindanao Deep," a story set in the Philippines, not only places an American traveler in an exotic locale, but also treats the theme of disease and medication explored in "The City of the Living."

Travel, as Susan Sontag points out in *Illness As Metaphor,* has come to be considered therapeutic: "to be cured, the patient has to be taken out of his or her daily routine" (36). Although Stegner's stories of travelers within the United States don't contradict the notion of travel as restorative, his fictional journeys to the Southern Hemisphere exhaust and weaken. Unlike Lucy Graham, the English war bride in "The View from the Balcony," who greedily absorbs American sunshine and wholesome food after the deprivations of wartime Europe, or Rusty (*né* Lionel) Cullen, who achieves manly vigor in the New World wild, Stegner's Americans abroad lose physical well-being. While the warmth of an Indiana summer "makes the corn grow," and Lucy Graham takes "the sun like medicine" (92, 93), the heat of the Philippines poses a threat: under a "vertical sun," "Manila Bay was congealed lead, with three rusty hulks jutting above the surface, not quite melted down" (361). The alien tropical landscapes of "Something Spurious from the Mindanao Deep" and "The City of the Living" harbor lurking enemies and are infused with menace.

In these thematically complementary stories, middle-aged American men confront an otherness of land and people that disturbs their image of themselves and destroys their illusions of safety in a world revealed as perilous. Fearing the "xenophobic germs" (376) that populate the Philippines, Burns in "Something Spurious . . ." uses illness to justify fortifying himself against experience with an array of totemic pills and capsules. Chapman, in "The City of the Living," bitterly aware of "the steady, unrelieved, incessant effort that it took in [Egypt] to stay alive" (521), realizes that neither the potions of science nor bureaucratic guarantees can permanently outwit mortality.

In Stegner's Manila, "The palms hung without stir in the red evening, the hulks were black on the molten water, the promontory of Bataan was a dark low silhouette against a salmon-colored sky" (369).

Against this backdrop, Robert Burns views himself and others anew. Stuck by the prospect of the Bay as by a "lurid" "surrealist painting," he puts himself in the picture, "metamorphosed" as a "shrouded Indian with feet like bird claws or like roots" (361). Catching sight of an "emaciated face reflected back at him from a dusky glass door," Burns doubts its and thus his own identity: the reflection "might be a caricature of his real face, or again it might be the face of beast or bird" (361).

The prevailing atmosphere of personal and political passion also disturbs his equilibrium. At once attracted and repelled by people who take more chances than he dares take, Burns perceives falsity both in their "overlively" emotional lives (364) and in the background of unrest and violence against which those lives are lived. "Filipinos lived for drama," he concludes; "if the Huks had not existed they would have had to be invented" (365). He holds himself aloof from the drama of Ramon Avellanos and Pacita Delgado. When Pacita stakes her life on winning her lover, Burns recognizes, however, that what he had apprehended as "falseness" was in fact "a more passionate reality" (370). It is, however, too late for Burns, debilitated by sickness and exile, to experience that passionate reality. Tellingly, he refuses to attend the cockfight, a symbolic folk drama, according to Avellanos, of the gambling spirit that characterizes the Philippines.

During the seven months of Burns's travels, he has covered much of the territory of what was once an "Empire": "Cairo, Alexandria, Karachi, Bombay, Bangalore, Hyderabad, Madras, Calcutta, Singapore, Bangkok" (361). Along the way, he has accumulated an impressive catalogue of ailments: "I have had hepatitis, a strep throat, mononucleosis, and two bouts of what is affectionately called Delhi Belly. All I need is a case of amoebic to set me right up.... I just don't have any resistance to strange bugs" (364). The more distance Burns covers over the world's space, the more he retreats in time. Once critical of "segregated compounds," he has become all too wearily willing to take refuge in bars or clubs that serve as "residual fortresses . . . where Europeans and Americans kept themselves aloof. . . . Nearing the end of his tour of duty, he was also nearing the rueful admission that East was East and West was West" (361–62).

Burns experiences travel, not as bracing and broadening, but as an ordeal that prompts withdrawal to the political and social evasions of an earlier and supposedly alien order. As Susan Sontag suggests, "illness" effects a change of nationality:

Everyone who is born holds dual citizenship, in the kingdom of the well and in the kingdom of the sick. Although we all prefer to use only the good passport, sooner or later each of us is obliged, at least for a spell, to identify ourselves as citizens of that other place. (3)

Burns has switched his allegiance from the "health" of democratic ideals of brotherhood to the traditional ills of prejudice and estrangement. He presents the spectacle of an erstwhile New World man retreating behind old fortifications to avoid encounters with "people . . . who were marked in his mind as unalterably different from himself" (366).

What will Burns take home besides a new and rueful sense of being "a fatigued stranger in a crowd not his own" (367)? The story's title suggests questionable souvenirs other than the wares offered by the story's emblematic embodiment of the racial other: the peddler of pearls from "the Mindanao deep." Haunted for a week by the persistent hawker of "phony" pearls (362), an exasperated Burns at last offers his nemesis "five pesos to disappear":

For a second they stood braced and squinting. Then the peddler shrugged. "Okay."
Smiling broadly, seeming to search Burns' face for some corroboration, he took the five pesos. The wind flapped his shirt tails. "Well, what the hell," he said, and emptied into Burns' palm the four polished bits of shell. Moving away, he threw his open hand into the air in cheerful, perhaps mocking, salute. (375)

In "Something Spurious from the Mindanao Deep," Robert Burns engages himself in a rhetorical relationship. The third-person narrative chronicles a dispirited inner debate that results in uncomfortable awareness of having missed out: "the mementos of his mission, like his relations with the people he met, too often turned out to be spurious or ambiguous, or forced upon him. The real thing eluded him, or he evaded it" (375). To assuage fatigue and fear of sickness and their attendant "wistful shame" (376), Burns seeks the solace of a gimlet, "characteristic drink of the Empire" (361), and the spurious protection of "pills and capsules" (376).

Robert Chapman, protagonist of "The City of the Living," also travels with a precautionary supply of medicine: "penicillin tablets, Empirin, sulfaguanidine, Dramamine against travel sickness, Chloromycetin and Aureomycin in case we got sick anywhere out of reach of medical care

143

and had a real emergency" (519). In this title story of the collection in which it originally appeared, the dreaded "emergency" occurs, and Robert Chapman, like Burns an American cultural ambassador, is saved from ruin by his "little kit of pills" (519). The danger he faces is all the more menacing in that it threatens not his own person but that of his child. In a hotel on the Nile, Chapman anxiously watches while his son suffers through the crisis of typhoid, cured at last by the Chloromycetin dutifully dispensed throughout the long night.

The displacement of sickness onto the beloved son means that Chapman remains in full possession of his senses, through which he can perceive illness, suffering, and death. Whereas Daniel is lost in disease, his father is quarantined in a silent fear that sharpens his sensory perceptions. He sees "the vague shape under the [mosquito] net," the stars in the "rich blue-black" sky, and his son's emaciated pain-wracked body and "wasted" face (514–15). He hears the "occasional dry clashing" of the palms (513) and "the rise and fall of the muezzin's cry" (521). He smells the "carbolic reek of disinfectant" (513) and "the inhuman poisonous stench of the sickness" (515). He feels the heat of his son's "fever through sheet and net and three feet of air" (514). He tastes "bile," and "the chlorine bite of the halazone tablets" in the water from his carafe (521).

During the solitary night-long ordeal during which he speaks to no one and realizes that there is no one to whom he can even write, Chapman is also forced into sharpened perceptions of himself. The glimpsed "sight of his own trapped eyes glittering was an intense, dreamlike plausibility until he realized that he was looking into a mirror" (516). From determined disbelief in the nightmare of his son's disease, he moves to desperate attempts to reassure himself with the guarantees of Western science and contemporary social organization. Driven by need of some activity to pass the terrible hours, he resorts to writing a check to pay an insurance premium, an endeavor that epitomizes the vanity of his attempts to achieve security. Casting his lot with insurance and the wonder cures so cynically regarded by the drug salesman of "The Traveler," Chapman attempts to reestablish contact with "the order and security of home" (518). "I believe in insurance," he recalls having said, and mentally reviews the comforting catalogue of his policies. The Chapman automobile is covered for "personal injury, property damage, collision, fire, theft," and the Chapman house for "window breakage, hail, wind, fire, earthquake, falling airplanes." As for the Chapman body, it is protected "anywhere in the world" by "medical and hospital plans"

(519). Recalling the "little kit of pills" brought from home and now put to desperate use, Chapman dwells on these consolations until he goes to wash his face and so confronts again his own "shadowed eyes in the mirror" (519).

In European and North American culture, "medical thought," as Foucault has observed, "is fully engaged in the philosophical status of man" (198). Making the individual both "subject and object of his own knowledge," modern medicine binds human beings more rather than less closely to their own "finitude" (197). Constantly evoking and yet exorcising death, modern medicine "reminds" human beings of both mortality and "that technical world that is the armed, positive, full form of [their] finitude" (198). Stegner's Robert Chapman at once experiences and observes a dire threat to the flesh of his own flesh; he thus becomes "subject and object of his own knowledge." The chemical potions that he duly administers to stave off death serve to sharpen his realization of what Foucault terms "finitude"; catching sight of his own "shadowed eyes" in the mirror, he is recalled to an awareness of mortality. The vivid dream of death that follows this second view of himself awakens Chapman to the harsh realities measured by the hands of his watch and the thermometer's mercury.

Frustrated by a helplessness that is rendered all the keener by the knowledge that promises remedy, Chapman resorts to falsifying his perception of the right-angled pattern of the tiled bathroom in the hope of controlling dreaded disorder: "squinting or widening his eyes," he forces the tiles to spin out of their order and then back again:

> He held the squares firmly in focus for a minute, stretched them, let them spin, brought them back under the discipline of will and eye, relaxed again and let them spin, enjoying the control he had of them and of himself. (520–21)

Hypnotized into a last period of uneasy sleep, Chapman wakes to the story's final reflected self-image and a resulting projection of frustration onto the alien landscape: "He looked at his haggard, smudged face in the mirror and he hated Egypt with a kind of ecstasy" (521).

Egypt, engaged in a perpetual struggle with poverty and disease, challenges Western complacencies about safety, health, and death: Chapman stands amazed at "the effort, the steady, unrelieved, incessant effort that it took in this place to stay alive" (521). The threat he perceives to be posed by the place is one of infection—of trachoma, bilharziasis, syphilis, tuberculosis, cholera, and typhoid. Such danger cannot be countered with courage and manliness; it must be fought by manufactured drugs and disinfectants. Just before dawn, Chapman discovers the pills to have done their work; Daniel is sleeping normally, freed from the wasting fever. Once he is "Safe, relieved of anxiety, reassured, rescued" (523), Chapman can begin to learn the lessons that Egypt can teach. He looks with new insight (soon aided by binoculars) on "the river that when they first came had seemed to him a dirty, mud-banked sewer":

> It came down grandly, one of the really mighty rivers, pouring not so much out of the heart of the continent as out of all backward time, and in its yellow water it carried the rich silt for delta cotton fields, the bilharzia worms to infect the sweating fellahin at the ditch heads, the sewage and the waste, the fecundity, the feculence. The river was literally Egypt. (523)

From the panorama of the Nile and its creatures, Chapman comes to focus on one boy who, in a corner of the hotel garden, removes his clothes, washes himself, and prays. "A skinny, one-eyed boy with a horizon no wider than the garden he worked in," the praying youth is nonetheless "not pathetic or repulsive or ridiculous"; he is rather "completely natural." Having linked fecundity with feculence, Chapman can posit the connection of life and death. "Whatever he is praying to has more death in it than anything we know. Maybe it had more life too" (525). His own prayers, the American realizes, are addressed to lesser deities:

> He had been doing something like praying all night, praying to modern medicine, propitiating science, purifying himself with germicides, placating the germ theory of disease. But suppose he had prayed in thanksgiving, where would he have directed his prayer? Not to God, not to Allah, not to the Nile or any of its creature-gods or the deities of light. To some laboratory technician in a white coat. To the Antibiotic God. For the first time it occurred to him what the word "antibiotic" really meant. (525)

Chapman's tale, unlike the story of Robert Burns, does not end in inadequacy. Like Burns, Chapman has grasped that something is missing from his life, something amiss in his philosophy. But whereas Burns shrinks from risk and allows sickness to become a part of his nature,

146

Chapman transcends disease by accepting mortality. In a state of "rebellious, wistful shame" at his own fear and weakness (376), Burns will take home souvenirs that embody his journey's failure: the "fake" Mindanao pearls and a "little figurine of the goddess Lakshmi," that he considers equally "spurious" (366). Chapman, on the other hand, has purchased wisdom in the shape of a "vulture-headed" figure that is at once harbinger of death and image of "Mut, the Lady of Thebes, the Mother of the World" (525). Whereas "Something Spurious from the Mindanao Deep" illustrates the inadequacy of man-made nostrums, Stegner has wisely placed last in his *Collected Stories* "The City of the Living," a text that teaches that acceptance of mortality is necessary to validate the journey of life.

Works Cited

Foucault, Michel. *The Birth of the Clinic: An Archaeology of Medical Perception.* 1963. Trans. A. M. Sheridan Smith. New York: Vintage, 1975.

Sontag, Susan. *Illness as Metaphor.* New York: Farrar, 1978.

Stegner, Wallace. *The City of the Living and Other Stories.* 1956. Freeport, NY: Books for Libraries P, 1969.

———. *Collected Stories of Wallace Stegner.* New York: Random. 1990.

James Ellis

In one of the few critical essays to appear on Wallace Stegner, Robert Canzoneri has touched briefly on "the life-death and civilized-natural themes" in the stories of *The City of the Living*. Drawing particular attention to "Maiden in a Tower," he points to the story as an example of Stegner's concern with the inability to love.[1] Set in Salt Lake City, "Maiden in a Tower" treats the return of Kimball Harris to the scene of his early manhood and, as a consequence, his confrontation with the truth of his own sexual failure twenty-five years before—a confrontation that leads him to the discovery of self.

The story is structured upon an extended metaphor of life-in-death and death-in-life, Stegner elaborating upon this metaphor through the use of literary allusion. The story also depends for its effect upon a dual comparison, one between the two worlds of Kimball Harris—his youth in the late 1920's juxtaposed with his maturity in the early 1950's—and a second between the characters of the story and an assemblage of literary and mythical figures. Though a majority of the literary-mythical references are drawn from classical antiquity, the two works that make most explicit the meaning of the sexual failure of Kimball Harris are William Blake's *The Marriage of Heaven and Hell* and Goethe's *Faust*.

Returning to Salt Lake City to arrange for the funeral of his last near relative, an eighty-three-year-old aunt, Kimball Harris feels revived by his return. He is charmed to find the city much as he has remembered it from the late 1920's, still so remarkably clean and well-ordered by its Mormon monuments. But as soon as he sets about the business that has brought him back he is struck by the changes that have been wrought by time, discovering that the funeral parlor where are the remains of his aunt occupies the same house that formerly had contained the apartment of his first love, Holly.

"Wallace Stegner's Art of Literary Allusion: *The Marriage of Heaven and Hell* and *Faust* in "'Maiden in a Tower,'" reprinted from *Studies in Short Fiction* 17 (1980): 105–11. Copyright © 1980 by Newberry College.

Entering the funeral parlor Harris is met by a mortician, McBride, whose particular job it is to cosmetize the deceased so as to ensure that they look, in McBride's words, "nice [and] very sweet and peaceful."[2] Stegner describes Harris's indifference toward the "wax figure" of his aunt and then gives to Harris these concluding and dramatically ironic thoughts about his aunt: "All he could think as he looked at her was that she looked well-embalmed—but then she had probably been close to mummified before she died" (p. 72). Stegner's irony here anticipates Kimball Harris's later discovery of the deadness of his own life since Holly, the fact that he also—like his Aunt Margaret—has been "close to mummified" these past twenty-five years.

Stegner's irony continues in this same vein. Though Harris says that he does not "even feel the conventional disgust with young McBride," he is nevertheless amused at the mortician's pride in his work. Harris thinks to himself that McBride looked as though he "might have been left over from one of Holly's parties. He looked better equipped to write fragile verses than deal with corpses" (p. 71). Again Stegner's irony indicates that in judging McBride, Harris is in reality making a judgment upon himself, since he will discover that he too is a refugee from Holly's parties. Furthermore, Harris will discover that what he has done in his life since Holly has another parallel in McBride. For just as McBride's job is to create in the deceased life-in-death, so Kimball Harris—in fleeing from Holly's sexuality—has given himself up to death-in-life. In his own words—contrasting his life with that of Holly's—he had played it the other way, "not so much from choice as from yielding to pressures ..." (p. 81).

Feeling rather silly but nevertheless wanting very much to see again the third-floor apartment where Holly had once lived, Harris asks and receives permission from McBride to go on up. McBride warns him, however, that there is a woman "laid out" in the apartment—"presentable," according to McBride, if not yet made "nice." Intent as he is upon recovering the memory of Holly, Harris is still struck by the presence of this dead woman—a woman approximately his own age, "perhaps fifty." He notes her lying in a "simple black dress [with] ... a Navajo squash-blossom necklace around her throat," perceiving the necklace as "a remarkable piece of realism—perhaps something she had especially liked and had stubbornly worn even past the age when costume jewelry became her. It gave her a touching, naïvely rakish air" (p. 76).

Then, turning from the dead woman, Harris attempts to picture the romantic exoticism of Holly's apartment, remembering that it had always reminded him of "a Chinese whorehouse" with its "romantic gloom," its windows "always shrouded by artistically-frayed burlap," and the light "from lamps, most of them low on the floor and some of them at least with red globes." There was always, he remembered, "the smell of sandalwood" (p. 76). Here "reed-necked aesthetes, provincial cognoscenti, sad sexy yokels, lovers burning with a hard gemlike flame, a homosexual or two trying to look blasted and corroded by inward sin" consorted with "painters of bile-green landscapes, cubist photographers, poets and iconoclasts, scorners of the bourgeoisie, makers of cherished prose, dream-tellers, and correspondence school psychoanalysts" (p. 69). And it was always Holly, Harris remembers, who was the center of this assemblage of undergraduate poseurs.

Slightly embarrassed by the memory of these undergraduate literati, Harris turns his thoughts to Holly, recalling her in a succession of literary and mythical *femmes fatales.* Here again Stegner provides in his references to these goddesses not only a basis for a comparison of Holly to the ideal of feminine beauty but also an ironic reminder of Harris's own masculine failure with Holly. For what Proserpine, Circe, Lilith, Guenevere, Helen, and Aphrodite have in common is the power to coerce men into their service. But Kimball Harris, though he repeats the Judgment of Paris in choosing Holly over her roommates in their mock beauty contest, is only an "undergraduate Paris" who lacks the courage to abduct Holly from her tower. Preferring rather, like the knight in shining armor to whom he is compared, that his maiden remain innocent in her tower, Kimball Harris flees from the threat of her sexuality.[3]

His thoughts then turn to a particular Christmas morning when he had presented Holly a facsimile copy of *The Marriage of Heaven and Hell,* a volume that he remembers as "a mutinous book full of mottoes for their personalities and their times." She had kissed him then, rather suddenly and surprisingly, a kiss that he remembers as soft and sweet, "a kiss like a happy child's." It is at this point that Stegner joins the vision of William Blake with that of Goethe, for as Harris thinks back on this kiss, "he realized now that he had recalled that kiss before, waking or sleeping, and that the memory of it had acquired a kind of caption, a fragment of the world's wisdom contributed to his adolescent store by a returned Mormon missionary: 'Das ewig Weibliche zieht uns hinan,' that remembered moment said" (p. 75).[4]

This joining of Blake and Goethe is appropriate, for both *The Marriage of Heaven and Hell* and *Faust* argue that the glory of man is in the Contrary that is achieved by the interaction of the male and the female. Blake writes: "Without Contraries is no progression. Attraction and Repulsion, Reason and Energy, Love and Hate, are necessary to Human existence." Martin Nurmi's summary of Blake's vision as it is embodied in *The Marriage of Heaven and Hell* is instructive. He writes:

> [Blake] wants to free the creative vitality of life from the thralldom imposed upon it by the restrictive moral codes of the orthodox "religious," and to restore life to the original unity it had before the disjunctive categories of the abstract reasoners split it into destructive orders of "good" and "evil."
>
> Because *The Marriage* teaches that the essence of Human life is a vigorous yet complementary opposition, it does not merely attack "reason" and exalt "energy." It teaches that both reason and energy are necessary. It is a corrective, designed to open the eyes of the rational "angels" and restore them to their proper role as one of the contraries. Nor does such a restoration demand that the angels change their essentially rational and restrictive natures; Blake does not intend to do away with all bounds and restrictions, but only with those that merely hinder the positive acts necessary to life. In urging the restoration of the angels, he necessarily emphasizes the case for the "devils" of energy, and this emphasis may make *The Marriage* appear as an attack of "Hell" against "Heaven," in which no quarter is given. But such an emphasis was unavoidable, since it was the angels, self-righteously entrenched behind moral virtue, or "Heaven," who had to be dislodged; to dislodge them Blake found it necessary to apply the infernal corrosives of irony and exalt "Hell."
>
> The case for Hell, then, must be read within the context of the whole work. And even a moderately careful reading discloses that the main theme of *The Marriage* and the theoretical foundation of its ideas is the doctrine that both angels and devils are necessary, indeed, that they must be "married" within the larger unity of Human life.[5]

This union of "Reason and Energy," however, is beyond Harris. Rather like the puritan he is, he maintains a position akin to Blake's rational angels, safely entrenched in his orthodoxy and moralities incapable of marrying his masculinity to Holly's femininity.

Stegner's reference to *Faust* makes much the same kind of commentary on Kimball Harris as does *The Marriage of Heaven and Hell*. The frag-

ment from Goethe that Harris remembers—the final two lines of the
drama—is taken from the song of the Chorus Mysticus as Faust, at his
death, is borne aloft by a chorus of angels. These lines stand as a kind of
summary of the whole of *Faust*. The chorus Mysticus sings:

Alles Vergängliche	All in transition
Ist nur ein Gleichnis;	Is but reflection;
Das Unzulängliche,	What is deficient
Hier wird's Ereignis;	Here becomes action;
Das Unbeschreibliche,	Human discernment
Hier ist's getan;	Here is passed by;
Das Ewig-Weibliche	Woman Eternal
Zieht uns hinan.	Draw us on high.[6]

Of these difficult lines Hans Eichner writes: "As the published English versions show, this final passage is quite untranslatable. A para-
phrase might run as follows: " 'All that is transitory is merely symbolical;
here (that is to say, in the scene before you) the inaccessible is (symbolically) portrayed and the inexpressible is (symbolically) made manifest. The eternal feminine (i.e., the eternal principle symbolized by
woman) draws us to higher spheres.' "[7]

Faust, of course, represents the endless striving of man, and it is this
striving—this pursuit of the eternal feminine—that in the end saves him
from Mephistopheles. The forms that this striving will take are various,
but they are represented in part by the masculine desire of Faust for the
ideal of feminine beauty as it is represented in Helen. So intense is this
striving that Faust rescues Helen from the Underworld—bringing her
first to his medieval castle in Sparta and thence to Arcadia—so that his
love for her might be physically consummated. The sexual union of Faust
and Helen represents, moreover, a bringing together of contraries—a
union "of the drive and strength of the northern, romantic spirit" in Faust
with "the sensuous beauty of classic antiquity" as represented by Helen.[8]

Again, as was true also in regard to *The Marriage of Heaven and Hell*,
Kimball Harris is incapable of assuming the role of Faust to Holly's
Helen. Rather than daring to strive in accordance with his masculine,
Faustian nature toward a classical ideal, he flees from this challenge
until he finds the safer, more prudential life that he will come to recog-
nize as death-in-life.

The climax of the story—Harris's flight from Holly—is prepared for
in a scene in which Harris remembers an occasion when he and Holly

had looked down on what was then a "Peewee Golf Course where men in shirt sleeves, women in summer dresses, young couples loud with laughter, putted little white balls along precise green alleys and across precise circles of green artificial grass and over gentle and predictable bridges and causeways into numbered holes" (p. 76). A metaphor for a childish and safe life—a life for Blake's rational angels—this golf course serves Holly as the basis for a new type of golf course that she would construct—a golf course which would represent the danger implicit in life and the adult experience. Holly says: " 'Some day I'm going to build a miniature golf course with fairways six inches wide and rough all over the place. I'll fill the water holes with full-sized crocodiles and sow the sandtraps with sidewinders. How would it be to hide a black widow spider in every hole so that holing out and picking up your ball would earn you some excitement? What if you sawed the supports of all the little bridges nearly in two?' " (p. 77) Her description, I think, is so explicitly sexual in its double entendre that it requires no gloss. Kimball Harris will remember this metaphor when he confronts that time twenty-five years before when he failed Holly.

At that time, he had been alone with Holly "in a way they had seldom been." She had suddenly begun crying and had implored him to take her from her tower, telling him: " 'This is no good, I've got to, Kim, please!' " (p. 79) But Harris had fallen back on the pretenses that had sufficed until that time, muttering, as he says, consoling "inanities." Only when his hand was not stopped and he felt "almost with revulsion, how rigid and demanding [was] the nipple of her breast" did he realize that Holly had moved their relationship onto a more vital and dangerous ground. Harris, twenty-five years later, cannot remember—again, in his own words—"how he got away. She offered herself passionately in his memory, and that was all. The Peewee Golfer putting his little white ball up the little green alley of his youth came suddenly upon the sidewinder in the sandtrap, the crocodile in the artificial lake" (p. 80).

The memory of his innocence, Harris finds humiliating, recognizing that he had, in fact, been more the coward than the innocent. Seeing himself as "a fraud," he tries to find some excuse for not taking Holly, but no excuse is forthcoming. Stegner then invokes another reference to *The Marriage of Heaven and Hell* in describing the way in which Kimball Harris is forced to confront his inadequacy: "Like a bubble of gas from something submerged and decaying in deep water there rose to the surface of his mind one of Blake's proverbs of Hell that they had admired together that long-gone Christmas morning. It burst, and it said, 'Prudence is a rich ugly old maid courted by Incapacity' " (p. 81). The quotation of Blake would seem to link Kimball Harris with Incapacity and to identify his old Aunt Margaret as the Prudence that he has courted for these past twenty-five years. The result of this recognition is that he knows now that "his failure to take [Holly] when she [had] offered herself was one of the saddest failures of his life" (pp. 81–82).

At this moment the dead woman—Holly's surrogate and an embodiment of a lived life, a life given over innocently to adult experience—forces herself upon Harris. Pausing before leaving the room, he thinks of the woman, "how she had been transported and tampered with by McBride, and how further touches of disguise would complete her transfiguration from something real and terrible and lost to something serene, removed, bearable." For a moment he thinks himself grateful that he has been able to confront the fact of this woman's life as it is still revealed in her face. But as he leaves he finds himself attempting to make silent amends to the life force that he had betrayed here in Holly's room twenty-five years before, casting "a sick, apologetic glance around the room." He intends "to tiptoe out, but he heard, almost with panic, the four quick raps his heels made on the bare floor before they found the consoling softness of the stairs" (p. 83).

Stegner's concluding the story with this image provides a telling reminder of the scene twenty-five years before when Kimball Harris had also fled in panic. For the third floor of the funeral parlor, as Harris has noted, is carpeted only to the stairwell. The top floor and the floor of Holly's apartment remain covered in the parquetry of twenty-five years before. So the sound of his heels on the floor is at once both a reminder of his reality in the present and at the same time an evocation of the reality of the past, of Holly, and of the "rigid and demanding nipple of her breast." Then he had realized that he "had imagined wrong" about a woman's breast, in his innocence supposing it soft and consoling. Now, again fleeing from her apartment, he feels safe only when his feet find "the consoling softness of the stairs," where the plum-covered carpet of the funeral home eases the shock of reality. Thus, at the conclusion of the story, having once again been brought up against the hard fact of the reality of life and death, Harris once again—as he had twenty-five years before—flees "almost with panic," escaping to his more prudential, more consoling life.

Notes

1. Robert Canzoneri, "Wallace Stegner: Trial by Existence," *Southern Review,* 9 (1973), 819.

2. Wallace Stegner, "Maiden in a Tower," in his *The City of the Living* (Boston: Houghton, 1956), p. 72. Subsequent references will be to this edition and will be incorporated in the text.

3. In this connection Kimball Harris remembers a portrait of Holly in her gold gown and at the same time a rumor that there was also in existence, hidden away, a nude done by the same artist. At the time he remembers that he had been "malely offended, surprised that she would lower herself. . . ." This memory helps him to see that his own bohemianism of the 1920's had been a pose and that he had in fact been a puritan. In the context of the world of classical allusions that works in the story, these two portraits represent, I suggest, the two guises of Aphrodite: Aphrodite Urania, representing purity and celestial love, and Aphrodite Pandemos, representing lust and sensual love.

4. When "Maiden in a Tower" was first published in *Harper's,* these two lines were misquoted as follows: "Das ewig Weibliche *fuehrt* uns hinan"—The Eternal Feminine *leads* us upward rather than *zieht, draws* us upward. The lines were corrected when the story was collected in *The City of the Living.* See *Harper's,* Jan. 1954, p. 81.

5. Martin K. Nurmi, *Blake's Marriage of Heaven and Hell* (1957; rpt. New York: Haskell House, 1972), pp. 25–26.

6. Goethe, *Faust,* trans. Walter Arndt, ed. Cyrus Hamlin, Norton Critical Edition (New York: Norton, 1976), p. 308.

7. Hans Eichner, "The Eternal Feminine: An Aspect of Goethe's Ethics," *Transactions of the Royal Society of Canada,* Series IV, Vol. IX (1971), 235–244. Rpt. in *Faust,* ed. Cyrus Hamlin, Norton Critical Edition (New York: Norton, 1976), p. 616.

8. Goethe, *Faust,* ed. R-M. S. Heffner, Helmet Rehder and W. F. Twaddell (Madison, Wisconsin: University of Wisconsin Press, 1975), II, 43 [Arkadien], (no page number).

J. M. Ferguson Jr.

Although not often anthologized, Wallace Stegner's "The Blue-Winged Teal" is one of the finer short stories in American literature to deal with what is perhaps its most prominent theme, the "initiation" theme. The story's twenty-year-old protagonist, Henry Lederer, undergoes an experience which makes him feel "as if orderly things were breaking and flying apart in his mind," but it is an experience from which he emerges with new knowledge of himself and, significantly, of the father from whom he is at first estranged.

This estrangement is in part the result of his father's having returned to the proprietorship of his "old failure of a poolhall," a malodorous basement-level establishment which Henry privately likens to Avernus, just ten days after the death of Henry's mother, as if for thirty years of respectable marriage "his wife had been the jailer and he was now released." Moreover, Henry cannot forgive his father for the affair he is having with a "red-haired woman who sometimes came to the poolhall late at night and waited on a bar stool while the old man closed up." Hostile toward his father and poolhall environment, Henry thinks of himself as "the alien son" who "must gravel" his father, a man of "many failures," when, on the Saturday evening when the story begins, he presents him with the nine ducks he has killed on a successful day's hunt. Yet by the following Sunday afternoon, when Henry takes his leave from his father at the story's end, he does so without "the cold command of himself that he had imagined in advance." He has perceived that he has himself been "sullen and morbid" and "a difficult companion," and he has discovered within himself understanding and compassion for the father to whom he had thought "he would not bend again toward companionship." Subtly and beautifully, through the repeated images pertaining to the hunt, and through the recurrent symbol underscored by the title of the story, the author has established grounds for the plausibility of the protagonist's self-discovery and change of attitude.

"Cellars of Consciousness: Stegner's "The Blue-Winged Teal," reprinted with permission from *Studies in Short Fiction* 14 (1977): 180–82. Copyright © 1977 by Newberry College.

Four times in the first ten paragraphs Henry is referred to as "a hunter" or "the hunter," suggesting that he is a hunter not only of ducks but of something more elusive (returning to the poolroom from the duck hunt, he realizes that he is "ready to be dead again"); he seeks to know the character of his father (whose eyes cannot "quite meet, not quite hold, the eyes of his cold son"), and he seeks his own identity. This last object of his search is further suggested when he tries to sleep Saturday night in the hotel room which he is sharing with his father: "his mind was out again in half a minute, bright-eyed, lively as a weasel, and he was helplessly hunted again from hiding place to hiding place." Although he is reluctant to meet Henry's eyes, his father has "restless, suspicious eyes that [seem] always looking for someone," and in what might be referred to as the recognition scene of the story, when he finally meets Henry's gaze in the backbar mirror, his eyes are twice described as "hound eyes," suggesting that he too, though sick and exhausted, is in his own way a hunter.

Among the ducks which Henry has killed is a blue-winged teal, "a drab little duck" which nevertheless reveals a "hidden band of bright blue" when John Lederer, the father, spreads its wing, an act which brings "sentimental moisture" to his eyes. Later, he again spreads the teal's wing and sees "the band of blue hidden among the drab feathers," and finally, in the climactic recognition scene, Henry notices that his father has "tacked two wings of a teal upon the frame of the backbar mirror, small, strong bows with a band of bright blue half hidden in them."

Against the "bright blue" which is "half hidden" in the duck's wings, the author has played the suggestive color red. When John Lederer first observes the spread wing of the teal he comments, "You can have all your wood ducks and redheads, all the flashy ones." His preference for the teal seems especially significant after we learn of his occasional companion, "the red-haired woman," whose "cheap musky perfume" taints his clothes when it touches them "like some gaseous poison," and whose hair is after all not genuine, being "unreal" or false. Red is introduced early in the story in the person of Navy Edwards, perhaps another of the flashy ones, for he not only wears a flashy silk shirt with pearl buttons but serves as "dealer and bouncer" for Max Schmeckebier, "a stingy, crooked, suspicious little man" who runs a "cheap" and evidently illegal game of blackjack in a room adjacent to the poolroom. When he places an arm on Henry's shoulder, Henry turns "to see the hand with red hairs rising from its pores."

While this realistic detail reinforces the theme of red with its conno-
tations of cheapness, falsity and flashiness, a later detail strengthens the
counterposed theme of blue. During the final poolhall scene, a young
patron who has been engaging in "abstracted whistling" at one of the
tables begins to sing about a girl named Annie and, significantly, "the
guy that she's been waiting for" (i.e., her true, genuine love), concluding "She told me that I'd know you by the blue of your eyes."

Finally, employing a device for overcoming his insomnia on the Saturday night in the hotel room, Henry wrestles, perhaps unconsciously,
with both colors at once: "Yellow [this first color perhaps picking up the
image of his father's 'sallow face'] and blue and red, spotted and
striped, he shot pool balls into pockets as deep and black and silent as
the cellars of his consciousness." This descent into deeper levels of consciousness is, of course, the archetypal pattern of experience in the initiation story, but it has seldom been managed as artfully, or within a
framework of associations as rich with suggestion.

These dark "cellars of his consciousness" are flooded with sudden
light for Henry in the final recognition scene. Catching him looking at
the wings tacked to the backbar mirror, John Lederer recalls that
Henry's mother had decorated a set of "plain white china" with blue-
winged teal: "Just the wings, like that. She thought a teal was about
the prettiest little duck there was." Henry watches his father's face
in the mirror, and he realizes with "a cold, skin-tightening shock that
the hound eyes were cloudy with tears." Overcome with emotion, the
father leaves the counter where the duck feed is taking place, but
Henry interprets "the anguished look his father had hurled at the mirror": "The hell with you, the look had said. The hell with you ... my
son Henry. The hell with your ignorance, whether you're stupid or
whether you just don't know all you think you know ... you know less
than nothing because you know things wrong." Among the things Henry
has known wrong is his father. Although his father is perhaps a failure,
there is hidden within his experience a "band of bright blue" which is
painful but beautiful to recall, even if the outward appearance of his life
is like the outward appearance of the "little drab duck," the teal.

Moreover, Henry has also known himself wrong, and he realizes now
that his own coldness, antipathy and lack of understanding is at least in
part the source of his father's "anguished look." With his new insight
comes at least a fleeting moment of reconciliation as Henry takes his
leave of his father: "He said it like a cry, and with the feeling he might
have had on letting go the hand of a friend too weak and too exhausted

to cling any longer to their inadequate shared driftwood in a wide cold sea." Ironically, he has earlier in the day "been for three hours in the company of a friend," a friend from whom he has borrowed money to leave his father, but at the story's end he has discovered the existence of a friendship far more profound.

Chronology

1909   Born February 18 at Lake Mills, Iowa.

1909–1914 Lived in Grand Forks, North Dakota, and Redmond, Washington.

1914–1920 Lived in East End, Saskatchewan, in the winters, attending grammar school, and on a homestead near the Montana border in the summers.

1920–1921 Lived in Great Falls, Montana, and attended junior high school.

1921   Family moved to Salt Lake City, Utah, where they lived in 20 houses over the next 10 years. Wallace attended East High School.

1927   Graduated from high school and entered University of Utah at age 16. Played varsity tennis. Writing talent recognized by several professors, including novelist Vardis Fisher. Became editor of university literary magazine.

1930   Graduated from the University of Utah and took fellowship at the University of Iowa, where he became a teaching assistant and submitted three short stories for his master's thesis.

1932   Enrolled in a doctoral program at the University of California at Berkeley.

1933   Left Berkeley when his mother's cancer became worse and family moved from Los Angeles to Salt Lake City, where his mother died.

1934   Continued studies toward Ph.D. in American literature at University of Iowa and took full-time teaching job at Augustina College in Rock Island, Illinois. Married fellow graduate student Mary Stuart Page on September 1. First professional publication of a short story, "Pete and Emil."

1935   Took job as instructor at University of Utah and finished dissertation on Clarence Earl Dutton, surveyor of the West and naturalist.

1937   Son Page born January 31. Gained first literary success with publication of *Remembering Laughter* which won the Little, Brown novelette prize of $2,500. Began teaching at University of Wisconsin and started writing *The Big Rock Candy Mountain*.

1938   Joined staff at Bread Loaf Writers Conference, where he began friendships with Bernard DeVoto and Robert Frost.

1939   Father committed suicide in Salt Lake City. Appointed Briggs-Copeland Fellow at Harvard and began teaching in writing program there.

1940   *On a Darkling Plain*, first full-length novel, published.

1941   *Fire and Ice* (novel) published.

1942   *Mormon Country* (regional history and description) published. "Two Rivers" won Second Prize, O. Henry Memorial Short Story Awards.

1943   *The Big Rock Candy Mountain* (novel) published.

1945   Took leave from Harvard and went to work on *One Nation* for *Look* magazine. Shared Anisfield-Wolfe Award and received Houghton Mifflin Life-In-America Award for *One Nation* (a series of essays on discrimination and prejudice in the United States). Appointed Professor of English and Director of the Creative Writing Program at Stanford University.

1949   Built home in Los Altos Hills, California.

1950   First Prize, O. Henry Memorial Short Story Award, for "The Blue-Winged Teal." *The Preacher and the Slave* (novel) and *The Women on the Wall* (first story collection) published. Took around-the-world tour sponsored by Rockefeller Foundation.

1951   *The Writer in America* (essays) published.

1953   Took trip to discover the history of his childhood region in Saskatchewan.

1954   *Beyond the Hundredth Meridian: John Wesley Powell and the Second Opening of the West* (biography-history) published. "The City of the Living" won O. Henry Award. Traveled to Denmark and Norway to discover family roots.

1955   *This Is Dinosaur* (edited collection of essays) published.

1956   *The City of the Living* (second collection of stories) published.

1960   Wrote "Wilderness Letter" (one of the most famous environmental declarations).

1961   Became Assistant to the Secretary of the Interior Stewart Udall. *Shooting Star* (novel) published. Wallace Page Stegner, grandson, born.

1962   *Wolf Willow* (history, memoir, and two short stories dealing with Saskatchewan) published. Began four years of service on National Parks Advisory Board.

1963   Canadian Historical Association Certificate of Merit awarded to *Wolf Willow*.

1964   *The Gathering of Zion* (history), which won American Association for State and Local History Award of Merit, published. "Carrion Spring" won O. Henry Award.

1965   Elected fellow of American Academy of Arts and Sciences.

1967   *All the Little Live Things* (novel) published.

1969   *The Sound of Mountain Water* (first collection of essays) published. Elected member of National Institute of Arts and Letters.

1971   Retired from Stanford as Jackson E. Reynolds Professor of Humanities and Director of the Creative Writing Program. *Angle of Repose* (novel) published.

1972   Won Pulitzer Prize for Fiction for *Angle of Repose*.

1974   *The Uneasy Chair: A Biography of Bernard DeVoto* published.

1975   *The Letters of Bernard DeVoto* published.

1976   *The Spectator Bird* (novel) published.

1977   Won National Book Award for Fiction for *The Spectator Bird*.

1979   *Recapitulation* (novel) published.

1980   First recipient from *Los Angeles Times* of Robert Kirsh Award for Life Achievement.

1981   *American Places* (second collection of essays—with Page Stegner and photos by Eliot Porter) published.

1982   *One Way to Spell Man* (third collection of essays) published.

1987   *Crossing to Safety* (novel) and *The American West as Living Space* (fourth collection of essays) published.

1988   *On the Teaching of Creative Writing* (essays) published.

1990   *Collected Stories of Wallace Stegner* published.

1992   *Where the Bluebird Sings to the Lemonade Springs: Living and Writing in the West* (fifth collection of essays) published.

1993   Wallace Stegner died April 12 as a result of injuries sustained in an auto accident in Santa Fe, New Mexico, where he had gone to accept an award.

Selected Bibliography

Primary Works

Story Collections

The Women on the Wall. Boston: Houghton Mifflin Company, 1948.
The City of the Living. Boston: Houghton Mifflin Company, 1956.
The Collected Stories of Wallace Stegner. New York: Random House, Inc., 1990.

Uncollected Short Fiction

"Pete and Emil." *Salt Lake Tribune,* December 9, 1934.
"Saskatchewan Idyll." *Monterey Beacon,* June 29, 1935, 8–9.
"Home to Utah." *Story* 9 (August 1936): 28–42.
"Bloodstain." *American Prefaces* 2 (Summer 1937): 150–53.
"The Dam Builder." *Frontier and Midland* 17 (Summer 1937): 231–36.
"Fish." *Intermountain Review* 2, no. 1 (Summer 1937): 1.
"The Two Wives." *Redbook* 72 (July 1938).
"Remembering Laughter." *Redbook* 71 (September 1937). Also published as
    novelette: Boston: Little Brown and Company, 1937.
"The Potter's House." *American Prefaces* 3 (Summer 1938). Also published as
    novelette: Muscatine, Iowa: The Prairie Press, 1938.
"The Noise Outside." *Redbook* 73 (January 1939).
"One Last Wilderness." *Scribner's* 105 (January 1939).
"Clash by Night." *Redbook* 73 (November 1939): 131–62. (Abridged version of
    On a Darkling Plain [New York: Harcourt, Brace and Company, 1940].)
"One Thing at a Time." *Collier's* 106 (October 26, 1940).
"Say It with Flowers." *Mademoiselle* 12 (June 1941).
"The Four Mules of God." *Decision* 2 (October 1941): 19–23.
"The Turtle at Home." *Atlantic* 171, no. 4 (April 1943). Reprinted as "My Pet
    Achilles, the Amusing Turtle." *Reader's Digest* 42, no. 254 (June 1943):
    24–26.
"The Paradise Hunter." Parts 1 and 2. *Redbook* 82 (August 1943); 82 (September 1943).
"The House on Cherry Creek." *Collier's* 116, August 11, 1945, 16–17.
"Admirable Crichton." *New Yorker,* June 15, 1946. Reprinted in *Opinions and Attitudes in the Twentieth Century,* ed. Stewart Morgan. New York: The Ronald

Press Company, 1948, 66–72.

"Life Class." *Nugget* (July 1956).

"Genesis." *Contact* 2 (April 1959): 85–167. Also published as novelette in *Wolf Willow* (New York: The Viking Press, 1962).

"All the Little Live Things." *Mademoiselle* 49 (May 1959). Expanded into a novel of the same title (New York: The Viking Press, 1967).

"Indoor-Outdoor Living." *Pacifica* (Demonstration Issue September 1959): 16–23.

"The Wolfer." *Harper's* 219 (October 1959): 53–61.

"Chapter 13." *Contact* 2 (February 1961): 116–22. Excerpted chapter from *A Shooting Star* (New York: The Viking Press, 1961).

"Carrion Spring." *Esquire* 58, no. 4 (October 1962). Also published in *Wolf Willow*.

"Angle of Repose." *McCall's* 98 (April 1971): 103–10. Excerpted from the novel of the same title: Garden City, N.Y.: Doubleday & Company, Inc. 1971.

"Amicitia." *Sequoia* 31 (Centennial Issue 1987): 16–25.

Critical Essays on Short Fiction and Discussions of Writing Fiction

"Truth and Faking in Fiction." *Writer* 53 (February 1940): 40–43.

"The Making of Fiction." *Rocky Mountain Review* 6 (Fall 1941).

"Shaping of Experience." *Writer* 55 (April 1942): 99–102.

"Advice to a Young Writing Man." *Pro Tem* 1 (November 1943): 1.

"Get Out of That Story!" *Writer* 56 (December 9, 1943): 360–62.

"New Climates for the Writer." *New York Times Book Review*, March 7, 1948.

"A Problem in Fiction." *Pacific Spectator* 3 (Autumn 1949): 368–75.

"Variations on a Theme by Conrad." *Yale Review* 39 (March 1950): 512–23.

"Fiction: A Lens on Life." *Saturday Review* 33, April 22, 1950.

"Writing as Graduate Study." *College English* 11 (May 1950): 429–32.

"The Teaching and Study of Writing." *Western Review* 14 (Spring 1950): 165–79.

"Literary Lessons Out of Asia." *Pacific Spectator* 5 (Autumn 1951): 413–19.

"Workshops for Writers." *Today* (January 1952): 15.

"The Jones Room." *Appreciation* 2 (Summer 1955): 9–10.

"What Besides Talent?" *Author and Journalist* 41 (March 1956).

"Yarn-Spinner in the American Vein." Review of Charles Neider's *The Complete Short Stories of Mark Twain*. *New York Times Book Review*, February 10, 1957, 1.

"To a Young Writer." *Atlantic* 204 (November 1959): 88–91.

"Introduction" to *Bret Harte, The Outcasts of Poker Flat and other Tales*, by Bret Harte. New York: The New American Library, 1961. Reprinted as "The West Synthetic: Bret Harte" in *The Sound of Mountain Water* (Garden City, N.Y.: 1969).

"To an Anonymous Admirer." *Sequoia* 7 (Spring 1962): 1–7.

"Creative Writer as an Image Make." *Writer* 76 (October 1963): 24.
Teaching the Short Story. Davis, Calif.: Davis Publications in English, 1966.
"On Censorship." *Arts in Society* 4 (Summer 1967): 281–99.
"Breadloaf in the '40s." *Middlebury College News Letter* 49 (Summer 1975): 30–31.
"The Writer's Sense of Place." *South Dakota Review* 13 (Autumn 1975): 49–52.
"Literary by Accident." *Utah Libraries* 18 (Fall 1975): 7–21.
"The Writer and the Concept of Adulthood." *Daedalus* 105 (Fall 1976): 39–48.
"Literary Life Anything But Romantic." *Intellect* 106 (September 1977): 107.
"Excellence and the Pleasure Principle." *Writing* 1, nos. 3-4 (1979): 4–9.
"On Steinbeck's Story 'Flight.' " Afterword to *"Flight" A Story by John Steinbeck.*
    43–52. Covelo, CA: The Yolla Bolly Press, 1984. Reprinted in *Where the Bluebird Sings to the Lemonade Springs* (New York: Random House, 1992).
"Haunted by Waters." In *Norman Maclean*, edited by Ron McFarland and Hugh Nichols, 153–60. Lewiston, ID: Confluence, 1988.
On the Teaching of Creative Writing. Hanover, New Hampshire: University Press of New England, 1988.

Secondary Works

Bibliography

Colberg, Nancy. *Wallace Stegner: A Descriptive Bibliography.* Intro. by James R. Hepworth. American Authors Series. Lewiston, Idaho: Confluence Press, Inc., 1990.

Biography

Benson, Jackson J. *Wallace Stegner: The Man and His Work.* New York: The Viking Press, 1995.
Rankin, Charles E., ed. *Wallace Stegner: Man and Writer.* Foreword by Stewart L. Udall. Albuquerque: University of New Mexico Press, 1996.
Willrich, Patricia Rowe. "A Perspective on Wallace Stegner." *The Virginia Quarterly Review* 67, no. 2 (Spring 1991): 240.

Autobiography

Stegner, Wallace. "Wallace Stegner." In *Contemporary Authors, Autobiography Series.* 9: 257–71. Detroit: Gale Research Co., 1989.

Interviews

Ferguson, Suzanne. "History, Fiction, and Propaganda: The Man of Letters and the American West: An Interview with Wallace Stegner." In *Literature and the Visual Arts in Contemporary Society,* edited by Suzanne Ferguson and Barbara Groselclose, 3–22. Columbus: Ohio State University Press, 1985.

Hepworth, James R. "The Art of Fiction CXVIII: Wallace Stegner." *The Paris Review* 32, no. 115 (Summer 1990): 58.

Stegner, Wallace and Richard W. Etulain. *Conversations with Wallace Stegner on Western History and Literature.* Revised edition. Salt Lake City: University of Utah Press, 1990.

Criticism

Ahearn, Kerry D. "Stegner's Short Fiction." *South Dakota Review* 4 (Winter 1985): 70–86.

Benson, Jackson J. "Finding a Voice of His Own: The Story of Wallace Stegner's Fiction." *Western American Literature* 29 (August 1994): 99–122. ("The Women on the Wall" and "Field Guide to Western Birds.")

———. "A Friendship with Consequences: Robert Frost and Wallace Stegner." *South Dakota Review* (Summer 1996): 7–23. ("The Sweetness of the Twisted Apples," "The View from the Balcony," and "Saw Gang.")

Burrows, Russell. "Wallace Stegner's Version of the Pastoral." *Western American Literature* 25 (May 1990): 15–25. ("All the Little Live Things," "Coda: A Wilderness Letter," "Rediscovering America: 1946," *Spectator Bird, Angle of Repose, A Shooting Star, Crossing to Safety, The Sound of Mountain Water, Wolf Willow, A Shooting Star.*)

Canzoneri, Robert. "Wallace Stegner: Trial by Existence." *Southern Review* 9 (Autumn 1973): 796–827.

Eisinger, Chester E. "Twenty Years of Wallace Stegner." *College English* 20 (December 1958): 110–16. ("Beyond the Glass Mountain," "The Blue-Winged Teal," "Buglesong," "City of the Living," "The Colt," "Field Guide to the Western Birds," "Fire and Ice," "In the Twilight," "On a Darkling Plain," "The Potter's House," "The Preacher and the Slave," "Second Growth," "The Sweetness of the Twisted Apples," "View from the Balcony," "The Volcano," and "The Women on the Wall."

Ellis, James. "Wallace Stegner's Art of Literary Allusion: *The Marriage of Heaven and Hell* and *Faust* in 'Maiden in a Tower.' " *Studies in Short Fiction* 17 (Spring 1980): 105–11. Reprinted in this volume.

Ferguson, J. M. "Cellars of Consciousness: Stegner's 'The Blue-Winged Teal.' " *Studies in Short Fiction* 14 (Spring 1977): 180–82. Reprinted in this volume.

Flora, Joseph M. "Vardis Fisher and Wallace Stegner: Teacher and Student." *Western American Literature* 5 (Summer 1970): 121–28. Reprinted in *Critical Essays on Wallace Stegner.* Edited by Anthony Arthur (Boston: G. K. Hall & Co., 1982).

————. "Stegner and Hemingway as Short Story Writers: Some Parallels and Contrasts in Two Masters." *South Dakota Review* 30, no. 1 (Spring 1992): 104–19. Reprinted in this volume.

Lewis, Merrill and Lorene Lewis. *Wallace Stegner.* Boise State College Western Writers Series, no. 4. Boise, Idaho: Boise State College, 1972.

Robinson, Forrest G. and Margaret G. Robinson. *Wallace Stegner.* Twayne's United States Authors Series, no. 282. Boston: Twayne Publishers, 1977.

Zahlan, Anne Ricketson. "Cities of the Living: Disease and the Traveler in the Collected Stories of Wallace Stegner." *Studies in Short Fiction* 29 (Fall 1992): 509–15. Reprinted in this volume.

Reviews of Stegner Story Collections

CITY OF THE LIVING

Alpert, Hollis. "Dry Wine." *Saturday Review* 39, November 3, 1956, 17.

Butz, Robert C. "The Stanford Storyteller—a Prize Collection." *San Francisco Chronicle*, November 18, 1956, 24.

Davis, R. G. "Voices Speaking from the Lonely Crowd." *New York Times Book Review*, October 28, 1956, 6.

Duffy, Joseph M. Jr. "Between Distinction and Popularity." *Commonweal* 65, November 23, 1956, 213.

Fenton, Charles A. "Short Stories." *Yale Review* 46 (1957): 451–53.

Gray, James. "Stegner's Short Stories." *New York Herald Tribune Book Reviews*, November 4, 1956: 4.

Kobak, Jim. "Fiction." *Jim Kobak's Kirkus Reviews* (Kirkus) 24, August 15, 1956, 597.

Vanek, Edna, ed. "Fiction." *Booklist* 53, no. 7 (December 1, 1956): 176.

WOMEN ON THE WALL

Cleveland Public Library. *Cleveland Open Shelf*, March 1950, 8.

"Distinguished American Short Stories." *Christian Science Monitor*, Pacific edition, February 2, 1950, 11.

Feikema, Feike. "Some Tasty Samples of 'Candy Mountain.' " *Chicago Sun-Times*, January 9, 1950, 45.

Forrelly, John. "Brief Comment." *New Republic* 122 (March 13, 1950): 21.

Guilfoil, Kelsey. "Stories Too Often Make Little Point." *Chicago Daily Tribune*, January 8, 1950, 4.

Henderson, R. W. "Too Late for Last Issue." *Library Journal* 75 (January 15, 1950): 106.

Jackson, Joseph Henry. "New Stegner Stories." *San Francisco Chronicle*, January 4, 1950, 18.

Kobak, Jim. "Fiction." *Jim Kobak's Kirkus Review* (Kirkus) 17 (November 1, 1949): 611.

MacGregor, Martha. "A Fine Collection of Short Stories." *New York Post*, n.d.

Match, Richard. "Eighteen Stories by Wallace Stegner." *New York Herald Tribune Book Review* 26, no. 1 (January 1950): 4.

New York State Library. *Book Mark* 9 (April 1950): 161.

Peden, William. "Bruce, A Sensitive Boy, and Life." *Saturday Review of Literature* 33 (January 21, 1950): 17.

Pickrel, Paul. *Yale Review* 39 (Spring 1950): 5.

Salemson, Harold J. "Short Stories Range over Diverse Locales." *Dallas Morning News*, January 30, 1950, sec. 3.

Sylvester, Harry. "Regional Stories." *New York Times Book Review*, January 1, 1950, 15.

Wilson, Edmund. "Briefly Noted Fiction." *New Yorker* January 7, 1950, 80.

Wisconsin Free Library Commission. *Wisconsin Library Bulletin* 46 no. 1 (January 1950): 20.

Wexler, Beverly. "Books in Review." *The Trumpeteer* 4 no. 2 (February 1950): 7.

COLLECTED STORIES OF WALLACE STEGNER

Dowling, Tom. "Stegner's Stories are Admirable but Far from Lovable." *San Francisco Examiner*, April 27, 1990, C-8.

Garrett, George. "Wallace Stegner: Lessons of the Master." *Washington Post Book World*, April 1, 1990, 7.

Hepworth, James R. "A Crude Instrument, a Little Pigment and Some Stolen Time." *Bloomsbury Review* 10 (July 1990): 5.

Hooper, Brad. *BookList* 86 (January 15, 1990): 955.

Kimball, Clark. "Stopping Places on an American Journey." *Los Angeles Times Book Review*, April 15, 1990, 7.

Klinkenborg, Verlyn. "Writing the Land." *New Republic* 203 (August 20–27, 1990): 38–40.

Little, Charles. "Books for the Wilderness." *Wilderness* 53 (Summer 1990): 58–59.

Locy, Sharon. *America* 164, no.110 (March 16, 1991): 296.

Martin, Claire. "Stories Take a New Look at Realities: Wallace Stegner Gives Inventive Slant on Life." *Denver Post*, May 13, 1990, 8D.

Pollock, Sarah. "Wallace Stegner's Stops Along His Journey." *San Francisco Examiner*, March 25, 1990.

Rice, William. "Wallace Stegner's Tales of Cruelty and Kindness." *Chicago Tribune*, March 18, 1990, 7.

St. John, Edward B. *Library Journal* 115 (March 1, 1990): 118.

Seib, Philip. "A Careful Observer: Tales about Decent People Who Lead Quietly Heroic Lives." *Dallas Morning News*, June 3, 1990, 6J.

Shelnutt, Eve. "Social History: Stegner Focuses on 'Right Thinking.' " *Milwaukee Journal* March 25, 1990, 11E.

Steinberg, Sybil. "Forecasts: Fiction." *Publishers Weekly* 237 (January 26, 1990), 402.

Tyler, Anne. "The Outsider May Be You." *The New York Times Book Review*, March 18, 1990, 2.

Wakefield, Richard. "Stegner Casts His Long Gaze on our Endless Yearning." *Seattle Times*, June 3, 1990, K7.

White, R. T. *Choice* 28 (October 1990): 312.

Index

The Author

Jackson J. Benson is professor of English and Comparative Literature at San Diego State University. He has published 10 books on modern American literature, among them *The True Adventures of John Steinbeck, Writer*, which won the PEN-West USA Award for Non-Fiction, and *Wallace Stegner: His Life and Work*, which won the Evans Biography Award. He has twice been a fellow of the National Endowment for the Humanities, has received several awards for teaching excellence, and is on the editorial boards of two scholarly journals.

The Editors

Gary Scharnhorst is professor of English at the University of New Mexico, coeditor of *American Literary Realism*, and editor in alternating years of *American Literary Scholarship: An Annual*. He is the author or editor of books about Horatio Alger Jr., Charlotte Perkins Gilman, Bret Harte, Nathaniel Hawthorne, Henry David Thoreau, and Mark Twain, and he has taught in Germany on Fulbright fellowships three times (1978–1979, 1985–1986, 1993). He is also the current president of the Western Literature Association and the Pacific Northwest American Studies Association.

Eric Haralson is assistant professor of English at the State University of New York at Stony Brook. He has published articles on American and English literature in *American Literature, Nineteenth-Century Literature*, the *Arizona Quarterly, American Literary Realism*, and the *Henry James Review*, as well as in several essay collections. He is also the editor of *The Garland Encyclopedia of American Nineteenth-Century Poetry*.